Kitchen Aid Ice Cream Maker Cookbook 2025

Exclusive Frozen Treats with Your Stand Mixer: Homemade Recipes for Ice Creams, Yogurts, Gelatos, Sorbets, Mix-Ins & more Using the Attachment

Patrick Allen

MY SINCERE GRATITUDE TO YOU

Thank you for choosing this book and making it part of your culinary journey. Your trust in my recipes for the KitchenAid Ice Cream Maker means so much to me, and I am deeply grateful for your support.

This book is the result of countless hours of experimenting, and knowing these recipes will bring joy to your kitchen fills me with pride and gratitude. I hope they inspire creativity and excitement in your culinary adventures.

Your support fuels my passion and motivates me to keep exploring and sharing new ideas. Thank you for allowing my recipes to play a part in your journey.

As you explore these pages, I hope you find inspiration and create delicious memories. Happy creating and enjoying every moment!

With Love

Patrick Allen

This Cookbook Belongs to

_____

_____

_____

<u>About the Author</u>

Patrick Allen is a New York-based chef, author, and restaurateur who champions the idea that the right kitchen tools can transform cooking into a joyful and effortless experience.

With a passion for culinary innovation, Patrick has penned several renowned books on mastering kitchen devices to create mouthwatering recipes, making him a trusted voice for home cooks and professionals alike.

When not writing or exploring new recipes, Patrick can be found at his small upscale restaurant, where he combines his love for fresh ingredients and modern techniques to delight diners. His work reflects a deep commitment to simplifying and elevating everyday cooking.

He resides in New York City with his wife, two children, and their beloved dog.

Always Remember that:

A device is only as good as how you use it. may your kitchen be filled with creativity, joy, and delicious moments

CONTENTS

INTRODUCTION

Hello, I'm Patrick—a chef based in the bustling heart of New York City. My culinary journey has been filled with endless exploration, creativity, and, of course, a love for all things delicious. Over the years, I've found joy in creating recipes that bring people together, and nothing does that quite like a bowl of rich, creamy ice cream or a refreshing sorbet.

As someone who relies on my stand mixer daily, from whipping up dough to crafting desserts, I was thrilled to discover the KitchenAid Ice Cream Maker Attachment. It was the perfect addition to my kitchen arsenal—effortless to use, versatile, and seamlessly integrated into my routine. What once felt like a complicated process of churning and freezing ice cream by hand became an enjoyable, streamlined task. Now, creating frozen desserts isn't just convenient; it's a creative playground where flavors and textures come to life.

In this cookbook, I'll share some of my favorite frozen dessert recipes that have been tested, perfected, and loved by friends, family, and clients. Whether you're craving classic vanilla ice cream, an adventurous pistachio gelato, or a tangy mango yogurt, you'll find something here to spark your imagination.

This book is designed not only to teach but also to inspire. It's about celebrating the joy of making something from scratch and discovering how easy it is to create gourmet-quality frozen treats at home. With your KitchenAid Ice Cream Maker, you'll unlock a world of possibilities and elevate your dessert game to new heights.

Let's dive in and make magic happen, one frozen scoop at a time. Because when you craft something so special with your own hands, it's more than just dessert—it's pure joy.

Benefits of Using the KitchenAid Ice Cream Maker

The KitchenAid Ice Cream Maker Attachment is a game-changer for anyone who loves creating homemade frozen desserts. Here's why it stands out as an indispensable tool in your kitchen:

Effortless Integration with Your Stand Mixer

The ice cream maker attachment is the perfect complement if you already own a KitchenAid stand mixer. It transforms your mixer into a high-powered dessert machine, eliminating the need for a separate appliance. Simply attach, pour, and let your mixer do the work.

Homemade Quality with Professional Results

With this attachment, you can achieve a smooth, creamy texture that rivals store-bought ice cream. The design ensures even mixing and churning, giving you consistently excellent results every time. Whether it's a classic vanilla or a complex gelato, your desserts will have that luxurious, melt-in-your-mouth finish.

Versatility for Endless Creations

The possibilities are endless, from rich ice creams and silky gelatos to refreshing sorbets and tangy frozen yogurts. You can experiment with unique flavor combinations, incorporate seasonal ingredients, and customize every detail to suit your tastes or dietary needs.

Convenience and Ease of Use

The attachment is easy to assemble, use, and clean. Its pre-freezing bowl design allows for quick setup, while the churning paddle ensures consistent blending without manual effort. Making homemade frozen treats no longer feels like a chore.

Cost-Effective and Sustainable

Making ice cream at home helps you save money and reduce packaging waste. You also have full control over the ingredients—there are no preservatives, artificial flavors, or extra sugar.

Perfect for Any Occasion

If you're having a dinner party, celebrating something special, or want to enjoy a treat, the KitchenAid Ice Cream Maker lets you whip up something delightful in no time.

This attachment turns making frozen desserts into a fun and creative activity, rather than just a chore. It brings the craft of creating professional desserts right to your kitchen, making each scoop a display of your cooking talents.

Tips for Success: Mastering Your Stand Mixer and Attachment

Using the KitchenAid Ice Cream Maker Attachment is simple, but a few essential tips can help you get the best results each time. Use these tips to enjoy your frozen dessert experience fully:

Pre-Freeze the Bowl Properly

Always chill your ice cream base before you pour it into the bowl. A cold base makes churning easier and prevents the mixture from heating too fast, leading to creamier ice cream.

Chill Your Ingredients List

Always chill your ice cream base before pouring it into the bowl. A cold base helps the churning process and prevents the mixture from quickly warming the bowl, resulting in creamier ice cream.

Don't Overfill the Bowl

Avoid overfilling the freezer bowl. Leave enough space for the mixture to expand as it freezes and churns. Overfilling can lead to uneven freezing and a less-than-perfect texture.

Start the Mixer Before Adding the Mixture

Begin by setting the mixer to the suggested speed, typically stir or low speed, before adding the chilled mixture to the freezer bowl. This stops the mixture from freezing too fast against the sides of the bowl.

Monitor the Churning Time

Watch the churning process closely. It usually takes about 20 to 30 minutes for most ice cream mixtures to get to the right consistency. If the ice cream gets too thick, the paddle might have a hard time, so it's a good idea to stop before that occurs.

Use the Right Speed Setting

Stick to the recommended speed for your stand mixer model. Higher speeds can overwork the attachment or affect the texture of your ice cream.

Add Mix-Ins at the Right Time

Add mix-ins like chocolate chips, nuts, or fruit in the last few minutes of churning. This makes sure they are spread out evenly without interrupting the freezing process.

Work in Batches if Needed

When you have a lot to mix, split it into smaller portions. This keeps the bowl cold and ensures every batch is mixed just right.

Store Properly

After churning, put your ice cream in an airtight container immediately and freeze it for a few hours to firm it up. This last step improves the texture and taste.

Clean and Store with Care

Let the freezer bowl cool to room temperature before you wash it. Avoid using hot water, as it can harm the freezing liquid inside. After cleaning, dry it well and put it in the freezer for easy access later.

With these tips, you'll easily make frozen desserts with a professional texture and flavor, making your KitchenAid Ice Cream Maker a reliable kitchen helper.

Essential Ingredients List and Tools

Making great frozen desserts begins with using good ingredients and having the right tools. With some preparation, you'll have everything you need to craft ice creams, gelatos, sorbets, and more with your KitchenAid Ice Cream Maker Attachment.

Essential Ingredients List

1. **Dairy**

   - **Cream and Milk**: High-quality heavy cream and whole milk are the foundation of rich and creamy ice creams. For a lighter option, use low-fat milk or a combination of milk alternatives like almond or coconut milk.

   - **Half-and-Half**: This can be used as a substitute for cream to reduce fat without sacrificing creaminess.

2. **Sweeteners**

   - **Granulated Sugar**: Essential for sweetness and ensuring a smooth texture by lowering the freezing point.

   - **Brown Sugar**: Adds a hint of molasses flavor for a deeper, caramel-like sweetness.

   - **Honey, Maple Syrup, or Agave Nectar**: Great for natural sweetness and unique flavor profiles.

3. **Egg Yolks**

   - It is used in custard-based ice creams (French-style) for richness and a velvety texture. The yolks must be tempered to avoid curdling.

4. **Flavorings**

   - **Vanilla Extract or Bean Paste**: A staple for most recipes, pure vanilla provides the best flavor.

   - **Cocoa Powder and Chocolate**: Essential for chocolate-based recipes. Use high-quality options for superior results.

   - **Fresh Fruits**: Perfect for sorbets, fruity ice creams, and mix-ins. Choose ripe, flavorful produce.

   - **Spices and Herbs**: Experiment with cinnamon, cardamom, mint, or even basil for creative flavors.

5. **Stabilizers and Additives (Optional)**

   - **Corn Syrup or Invert Sugar**: Helps prevent ice crystals and keeps desserts soft.

   - **Gelatin or Agar-Agar**: Can be used for improved texture and stability.

Essential Tools

1. **KitchenAid Stand Mixer**

   - The backbone of your setup, the stand mixer powers the ice cream maker attachment with consistent and reliable performance.

2. **KitchenAid Ice Cream Maker Attachment**

- It comes with a freezer bowl and paddle to create smooth and creamy frozen treats.

3. **Mixing Bowls**

    - For preparing and chilling your base. Stainless steel bowls are especially effective at maintaining temperature.

4. **Whisks and Spatulas**

    - A whisk is essential for mixing ingredients smoothly, and a silicone spatula is perfect for scraping the bowl clean.

5. **Measuring Cups and Spoons**

    - Accurate measurements ensure consistency in flavor and texture.

6. **Airtight Containers**

    - Keep your frozen desserts in airtight containers that are safe for the freezer. This helps keep them fresh and prevents ice crystals from forming.

7. **Thermometer**

    - Useful for monitoring custard temperatures to avoid overcooking egg-based bases.

8. **Blender or Food Processor**

    - Great for puréeing fruits or creating smooth, uniform bases for sorbets and yogurts.

9. **Ice Cream Scoop**

    - A sturdy, high-quality scoop makes serving effortless and adds a polished touch to presentation.

10. **Freezer Thermometer (Optional)**

    - Ensures your freezer is at the optimal temperature for storing frozen desserts (0°F or below).

With these ingredients and tools ready to go, you can easily experiment with flavors and techniques, making the process of creating frozen treats enjoyable.

CHAPTER 1: ICE CREAM & MIX-INS

Classic Vanilla Bean Ice Cream

Time Needed to Prepare: 15 minutes (plus chilling time)
KitchenAid Time: 20–25 minutes
Servings: 8

Ingredients List

- 2 cups of heavy cream
- 2 cups of whole milk
- 3/4 cup of granulated sugar
- 1 vanilla bean, split and seeds scraped (or 2 teaspoons pure vanilla extract)
- 4 large egg yolks

Instructions

1. In a medium saucepan, combine the heavy cream, whole milk, and half of the sugar. Add the vanilla bean seeds and the pod (if using). Heat over medium heat, stirring occasionally, until the mixture is hot but not boiling. Remove from heat.

2. In a mixing bowl, whisk the egg yolks with the remaining sugar until pale and creamy.

3. Slowly add 1/2 cup of the hot cream mixture to the yolks, whisking constantly to temper the eggs. Gradually whisk the tempered yolks back into the saucepan with the remaining cream mixture.

4. Cook over medium-low heat, stirring constantly with a wooden spoon, until the custard thickens and coats the back of the spoon (170–175°F). Do not let it boil.

5. Strain the custard through a fine-mesh sieve into a clean bowl to remove the vanilla pod and any cooked egg bits. Stir in vanilla extract (if using) for added flavor.

6. Allow the custard to cool to room temperature, then cover and refrigerate for at least 4 hours or overnight until completely chilled.

7. Freeze your KitchenAid Ice Cream Maker bowl for 24 hours. Assemble the attachment, attach the dasher, and turn the stand mixer to "Stir" speed.

8. Pour the chilled custard into the frozen bowl and churn for 20–25 minutes until the ice cream reaches a soft-serve consistency.

9. Transfer the ice cream to an airtight container and freeze for 2–3 hours for a firmer texture before serving.

Nutritional Information (Per Serving)

- Calories: 270 | Carbohydrates: 20g
- Protein Content: 5g | Total Fiber: 0g | Fats: 20g

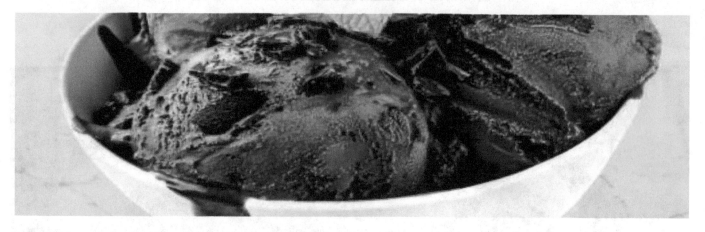

Rich Chocolate Fudge Ice Cream

Time Needed to Prepare: 20 minutes (plus chilling time)
KitchenAid Time: 20–25 minutes
Servings: 8

Ingredients List

- 2 cups of heavy cream
- 1 cup of whole milk
- 3/4 cup of granulated sugar
- 1/2 cup of unsweetened cocoa powder
- 1/2 cup of dark chocolate, finely chopped
- 4 large egg yolks
- 1 teaspoon pure vanilla extract

Instructions

1. In a medium saucepan, combine the heavy cream, whole milk, sugar, and cocoa powder. Heat over medium heat, whisking occasionally, until the mixture is hot but not boiling and the cocoa powder is fully dissolved.

2. Remove the saucepan from the heat and stir in the chopped dark chocolate until melted and smooth.

3. In a mixing bowl, whisk the egg yolks until pale and creamy. Slowly add 1/2 cup of the hot chocolate mixture to the yolks, whisking constantly to temper them.

4. Gradually whisk the tempered yolks back into the saucepan with the remaining chocolate mixture.

5. Return the saucepan to medium-low heat and cook, stirring constantly, until the custard thickens and coats the back of a spoon (170–175°F). Do not let it boil.

6. Strain the custard through a fine-mesh sieve into a clean bowl to remove any lumps. Stir in the vanilla extract.

7. Allow the custard to cool to room temperature, then cover and refrigerate for at least 4 hours or overnight until thoroughly chilled.

8. Freeze your KitchenAid Ice Cream Maker bowl for 24 hours. Assemble the attachment, attach the dasher, and turn the stand mixer to "Stir" speed.

9. Pour the chilled custard into the frozen bowl and churn for 20–25 minutes until the ice cream reaches a soft-serve consistency.

10. Transfer the ice cream to an airtight container and freeze for 2–3 hours for a firmer texture before serving.

Nutritional Information (Per Serving)

- Calories: 320 | Carbohydrates: 28g
- Protein Content: 6g | Total Fiber: 3g | Fats: 23g

Strawberry Swirl Ice Cream

Time Needed to Prepare: 25 minutes (plus chilling time)
KitchenAid Time: 20–25 minutes
Servings: 8

Ingredients List

- 2 cups of heavy cream
- 1 cup of whole milk
- 3/4 cup of granulated sugar
- 4 large egg yolks
- 1 teaspoon pure vanilla extract
- 1 1/2 cups of fresh strawberries, hulled and chopped
- 1/4 cup of granulated sugar (for the strawberry swirl)
- 1 tablespoon of lemon juice

Instructions

1. In a medium saucepan, combine the heavy cream, whole milk, and 3/4 cup of sugar. Heat over medium heat, stirring occasionally, until hot but not boiling. Remove from heat.
2. In a mixing bowl, whisk the egg yolks until pale and creamy. Slowly add 1/2 cup of the hot cream mixture to the yolks, whisking constantly to temper them.
3. Gradually whisk the tempered yolks back into the saucepan with the remaining cream mixture.
4. Return the saucepan to medium-low heat and cook, stirring constantly, until the custard thickens and coats the back of a spoon (170–175°F). Do not let it boil.
5. Strain the custard through a fine-mesh sieve into a clean bowl to remove any lumps. Stir in the vanilla extract.
6. Allow the custard to cool to room temperature, then cover and refrigerate for at least 4 hours or overnight until completely chilled.
7. In a small saucepan, combine the chopped strawberries, 1/4 cup of sugar, and lemon juice. Cook over medium heat, stirring occasionally, until the strawberries break down and form a syrupy mixture (about 10 minutes). Allow to cool completely, then refrigerate until ready to use.
8. Freeze your KitchenAid Ice Cream Maker bowl for 24 hours. Assemble the attachment, attach the dasher, and turn the stand mixer to "Stir" speed.
9. Pour the chilled custard into the frozen bowl and churn for 20–25 minutes until the ice cream reaches a soft-serve consistency.
10. Spoon half of the churned ice cream into an airtight container, drizzle with half of the strawberry syrup, and gently swirl with a knife. Repeat with the remaining ice cream and syrup.
11. Freeze the ice cream for 2–3 hours for a firmer texture before serving.

Nutritional Information (Per Serving)

- Calories: 290 | Carbohydrates: 26g
- Protein Content: 5g | Total Fiber: 1g | Fats: 21g

Salted Caramel Delight Ice Cream

Time Needed to Prepare: 30 minutes (plus chilling time)
KitchenAid Time: 20–25 minutes
Servings: 8

Ingredients List

- 2 cups of heavy cream
- 1 cup of whole milk
- 3/4 cup of granulated sugar
- 1/4 cup of water
- 1/4 cup of salted butter, cubed
- 1 teaspoon sea salt (plus extra for garnish, optional)
- 4 large egg yolks
- 1 teaspoon pure vanilla extract

Instructions

1. In a medium saucepan, combine the sugar and water over medium heat. Stir gently until the sugar dissolves, then increase the heat to medium-high and cook without stirring until the mixture turns a deep amber color (about 8–10 minutes).

2. Remove from heat and carefully whisk in the butter until fully incorporated. Gradually whisk in 1 cup of the heavy cream (be cautious, as it may splatter). Stir in the sea salt and set aside to cool slightly.

3. In a separate saucepan, combine the remaining 1 cup of heavy cream and whole milk. Heat over medium heat until hot but not boiling. Remove from heat.

4. In a mixing bowl, whisk the egg yolks until pale and creamy. Slowly add 1/2 cup of the warm milk mixture to the yolks, whisking constantly to temper them.

5. Gradually whisk the tempered yolks back into the saucepan with the milk mixture. Stir in the caramel sauce.

6. Return the saucepan to medium-low heat and cook, stirring constantly, until the custard thickens and coats the back of a spoon (170–175°F). Do not let it boil.

7. Strain the custard through a fine-mesh sieve into a clean bowl to remove any lumps. Stir in the vanilla extract.

8. Allow the custard to cool to room temperature, then cover and refrigerate for at least 4 hours or overnight until thoroughly chilled.

9. Freeze your KitchenAid Ice Cream Maker bowl for 24 hours. Assemble the attachment, attach the dasher, and turn the stand mixer to "Stir" speed.

10. Pour the chilled custard into the frozen bowl and churn for 20–25 minutes until the ice cream reaches a soft-serve consistency.

11. Transfer the ice cream to an airtight container and freeze for 2–3 hours for a firmer texture before serving. Garnish with a sprinkle of sea salt if desired.

Nutritional Information (Per Serving)

- Calories: 320 | Carbohydrates: 28g
- Protein Content: 5g | Total Fiber: 0g | Fats: 24g

Mint Chocolate Chip Ice Cream

Time Needed to Prepare: 20 minutes (plus chilling time)
KitchenAid Time: 20–25 minutes
Servings: 8

Ingredients List

- 2 cups of heavy cream
- 1 cup of whole milk
- 3/4 cup of granulated sugar
- 4 large egg yolks
- 1 teaspoon pure peppermint extract
- 1/2 teaspoon vanilla extract
- 2–3 drops green food coloring (optional)
- 3/4 cup of semisweet chocolate chips or chunks

Instructions

1. In a medium saucepan, combine the heavy cream, whole milk, and sugar. Heat over medium heat, stirring occasionally, until the sugar is fully dissolved and the mixture is hot but not boiling. Remove from heat.
2. In a mixing bowl, whisk the egg yolks until pale and creamy. Slowly add 1/2 cup of the warm cream mixture to the yolks, whisking constantly to temper them.
3. Gradually whisk the tempered yolks back into the saucepan with the remaining cream mixture.
4. Return the saucepan to medium-low heat and cook, stirring constantly, until the custard thickens and coats the back of a spoon (170–175°F). Do not let it boil.
5. Strain the custard through a fine-mesh sieve into a clean bowl to remove any lumps. Stir in the peppermint extract, vanilla extract, and food coloring (if using).
6. Allow the custard to cool to room temperature, then cover and refrigerate for at least 4 hours or overnight until completely chilled.
7. Freeze your KitchenAid Ice Cream Maker bowl for 24 hours. Assemble the attachment, attach the dasher, and turn the stand mixer to "Stir" speed.
8. Pour the chilled custard into the frozen bowl and churn for 20–25 minutes until the ice cream reaches a soft-serve consistency.
9. During the last 5 minutes of churning, gradually add the chocolate chips or chunks to ensure they are evenly distributed.
10. Transfer the ice cream to an airtight container and freeze for 2–3 hours for a firmer texture before serving.

Nutritional Information (Per Serving)

- Calories: 310 | Carbohydrates: 25g
- Protein Content: 5g | Total Fiber: 1g | Fats: 23g

Cookies and Cream Ice Cream

Time Needed to Prepare: 20 minutes (plus chilling time)
KitchenAid Time: 20–25 minutes
Servings: 8

Ingredients List

- 2 cups of heavy cream
- 1 cup of whole milk
- 3/4 cup of granulated sugar
- 4 large egg yolks
- 1 teaspoon pure vanilla extract
- 1 cup of crushed chocolate sandwich cookies (such as Oreos)

Instructions

1. In a medium saucepan, combine the heavy cream, whole milk, and sugar. Heat over medium heat, stirring occasionally, until the sugar is fully dissolved and the mixture is hot but not boiling. Remove from heat.
2. In a mixing bowl, whisk the egg yolks until pale and creamy. Slowly add 1/2 cup of the warm cream mixture to the yolks, whisking constantly to temper them.
3. Gradually whisk the tempered yolks back into the saucepan with the remaining cream mixture.
4. Return the saucepan to medium-low heat and cook, stirring constantly, until the custard thickens and coats the back of a spoon (170–175°F). Do not let it boil.
5. Strain the custard through a fine-mesh sieve into a clean bowl to remove any lumps. Stir in the vanilla extract.
6. Allow the custard to cool to room temperature, then cover and refrigerate for at least 4 hours or overnight until thoroughly chilled.
7. Freeze your KitchenAid Ice Cream Maker bowl for 24 hours. Assemble the attachment, attach the dasher, and turn the stand mixer to "Stir" speed.
8. Pour the chilled custard into the frozen bowl and churn for 20–25 minutes until the ice cream reaches a soft-serve consistency.
9. During the last 5 minutes of churning, gradually add the crushed chocolate sandwich cookies, ensuring they are evenly distributed.
10. Transfer the ice cream to an airtight container and freeze for 2–3 hours for a firmer texture before serving.

Nutritional Information (Per Serving)

- Calories: 330 | Carbohydrates: 31g
- Protein Content: 5g | Total Fiber: 1g
- Fats: 22g

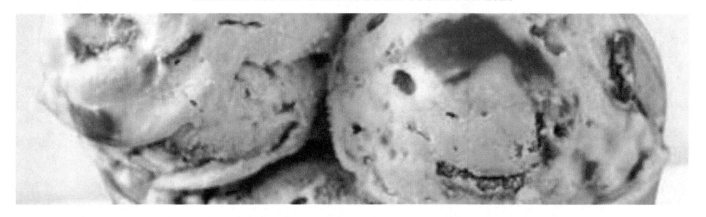

Peanut Butter Cup Ice Cream

Time Needed to Prepare: 25 minutes (plus chilling time)
KitchenAid Time: 20–25 minutes
Servings: 8

Ingredients List

- 2 cups of heavy cream
- 1 cup of whole milk
- 3/4 cup of granulated sugar
- 4 large egg yolks
- 1 teaspoon pure vanilla extract
- 1/2 cup of creamy peanut butter
- 1 cup of chopped peanut butter cups

Instructions

1. In a medium saucepan, combine the heavy cream, whole milk, and sugar. Heat over medium heat, stirring occasionally, until the sugar is fully dissolved and the mixture is hot but not boiling. Remove from heat.

2. In a mixing bowl, whisk the egg yolks until pale and creamy. Slowly add 1/2 cup of the warm cream mixture to the yolks, whisking constantly to temper them.

3. Gradually whisk the tempered yolks back into the saucepan with the remaining cream mixture.

4. Return the saucepan to medium-low heat and cook, stirring constantly, until the custard thickens and coats the back of a spoon (170–175°F). Do not let it boil.

5. Strain the custard through a fine-mesh sieve into a clean bowl to remove any lumps. Stir in the vanilla extract and creamy peanut butter until fully mixed and smooth.

6. Allow the custard to cool to room temperature, then cover and refrigerate for at least 4 hours or overnight until thoroughly chilled.

7. Freeze your KitchenAid Ice Cream Maker bowl for 24 hours. Assemble the attachment, attach the dasher, and turn the stand mixer to "Stir" speed.

8. Pour the chilled custard into the frozen bowl and churn for 20–25 minutes until the ice cream reaches a soft-serve consistency.

9. During the last 5 minutes of churning, gradually add the chopped peanut butter cups, ensuring they are evenly distributed.

10. Transfer the ice cream to an airtight container and freeze for 2–3 hours for a firmer texture before serving.

Nutritional Information (Per Serving)

- Calories: 360 | Carbohydrates: 29g
- Protein Content: 7g | Total Fiber: 1g | Fats: 25g

Coffee Espresso Crunch Ice Cream

Time Needed to Prepare: 25 minutes (plus chilling time)
KitchenAid Time: 20–25 minutes
Servings: 8

Ingredients List

- 2 cups of heavy cream
- 1 cup of whole milk
- 3/4 cup of granulated sugar
- 4 large egg yolks
- 2 tablespoons of instant espresso powder
- 1 teaspoon pure vanilla extract
- 3/4 cup of crushed chocolate-covered espresso beans

Instructions

1. In a medium saucepan, combine the heavy cream, whole milk, and sugar. Heat over medium heat, stirring occasionally, until the sugar is fully dissolved and the mixture is hot but not boiling. Remove from heat.

2. Stir in the instant espresso powder until fully dissolved.

3. In a mixing bowl, whisk the egg yolks until pale and creamy. Slowly add 1/2 cup of the warm cream mixture to the yolks, whisking constantly to temper them.

4. Gradually whisk the tempered yolks back into the saucepan with the remaining cream mixture.

5. Return the saucepan to medium-low heat and cook, stirring constantly, until the custard thickens and coats the back of a spoon (170–175°F). Do not let it boil.

6. Strain the custard through a fine-mesh sieve into a clean bowl to remove any lumps. Stir in the vanilla extract.

7. Allow the custard to cool to room temperature, then cover and refrigerate for at least 4 hours or overnight until thoroughly chilled.

8. Freeze your KitchenAid Ice Cream Maker bowl for 24 hours. Assemble the attachment, attach the dasher, and turn the stand mixer to "Stir" speed.

9. Pour the chilled custard into the frozen bowl and churn for 20–25 minutes until the ice cream reaches a soft-serve consistency.

10. During the last 5 minutes of churning, gradually add the crushed chocolate-covered espresso beans, ensuring they are evenly distributed.

11. Transfer the ice cream to an airtight container and freeze for 2–3 hours for a firmer texture before serving.

Nutritional Information (Per Serving)

- Calories: 310 | Carbohydrates: 28g
- Protein Content: 5g | Total Fiber: 1g | Fats: 22g

Cherry Cheesecake Ice Cream

Time Needed to Prepare: 30 minutes (plus chilling time)
KitchenAid Time: 20–25 minutes
Servings: 8

Ingredients List

- 2 cups of heavy cream
- 1 cup of whole milk
- 3/4 cup of granulated sugar
- 4 large egg yolks
- 8 oz cream cheese, softened
- 1 teaspoon pure vanilla extract
- 1 cup of cherry pie filling
- 1/2 cup of crushed graham crackers

Instructions

1. In a medium saucepan, combine the heavy cream, whole milk, and sugar. Heat over medium heat, stirring occasionally, until the sugar is fully dissolved and the mixture is hot but not boiling. Remove from heat.
2. In a mixing bowl, whisk the egg yolks until pale and creamy. Slowly add 1/2 cup of the warm cream mixture to the yolks, whisking constantly to temper them.
3. Gradually whisk the tempered yolks back into the saucepan with the remaining cream mixture.
4. Return the saucepan to medium-low heat and cook, stirring constantly, until the custard thickens and coats the back of a spoon (170–175°F). Do not let it boil.
5. Strain the custard through a fine-mesh sieve into a clean bowl to remove any lumps. Add the softened cream cheese and whisk until completely smooth. Stir in the vanilla extract.
6. Allow the custard to cool to room temperature, then cover and refrigerate for at least 4 hours or overnight until thoroughly chilled.
7. Freeze your KitchenAid Ice Cream Maker bowl for 24 hours. Assemble the attachment, attach the dasher, and turn the stand mixer to "Stir" speed.
8. Pour the chilled custard into the frozen bowl and churn for 20–25 minutes until the ice cream reaches a soft-serve consistency.
9. During the last 5 minutes of churning, gradually add the cherry pie filling and crushed graham crackers, ensuring they are gently swirled and evenly distributed.
10. Transfer the ice cream to an airtight container and freeze for 2–3 hours for a firmer texture before serving.

Nutritional Information (Per Serving)

- Calories: 340 | Carbohydrates: 30g
- Protein Content: 6g | Total Fiber: 1g | Fats: 24g

Pistachio Dream Ice Cream

Time Needed to Prepare: 30 minutes (plus chilling time)
KitchenAid Time: 20–25 minutes
Servings: 8

Ingredients List

- 2 cups of heavy cream
- 1 cup of whole milk
- 3/4 cup of granulated sugar
- 4 large egg yolks
- 1/2 teaspoon pure almond extract
- 1 teaspoon pure vanilla extract
- 1/2 cup of pistachio paste
- 1/2 cup of chopped pistachios

Instructions

1. In a medium saucepan, combine the heavy cream, whole milk, and sugar. Heat over medium heat, stirring occasionally, until the sugar is fully dissolved and the mixture is hot but not boiling. Remove from heat.

2. In a mixing bowl, whisk the egg yolks until pale and creamy. Slowly add 1/2 cup of the warm cream mixture to the yolks, whisking constantly to temper them.

3. Gradually whisk the tempered yolks back into the saucepan with the remaining cream mixture.

4. Return the saucepan to medium-low heat and cook, stirring constantly, until the custard thickens and coats the back of a spoon (170–175°F). Do not let it boil.

5. Strain the custard through a fine-mesh sieve into a clean bowl to remove any lumps. Stir in the pistachio paste, almond extract, and vanilla extract until smooth and well mixed.

6. Allow the custard to cool to room temperature, then cover and refrigerate for at least 4 hours or overnight until thoroughly chilled.

7. Freeze your KitchenAid Ice Cream Maker bowl for 24 hours. Assemble the attachment, attach the dasher, and turn the stand mixer to "Stir" speed.

8. Pour the chilled custard into the frozen bowl and churn for 20–25 minutes until the ice cream reaches a soft-serve consistency.

9. During the last 5 minutes of churning, gradually add the chopped pistachios, ensuring they are evenly distributed.

10. Transfer the ice cream to an airtight container and freeze for 2–3 hours for a firmer texture before serving.

Nutritional Information (Per Serving)

- Calories: 350 | Carbohydrates: 28g
- Protein Content: 7g | Total Fiber: 2g | Fats: 26g

Lemon Meringue Pie Ice Cream

Time Needed to Prepare: 35 minutes (plus chilling time)
KitchenAid Time: 20–25 minutes
Servings: 8

Ingredients List

- 2 cups of heavy cream
- 1 cup of whole milk
- 3/4 cup of granulated sugar
- 4 large egg yolks
- 1/2 cup of lemon curd (store-bought or homemade)
- 1 teaspoon pure vanilla extract
- 1 cup of crushed graham crackers
- 1 cup of mini marshmallows or meringue pieces

Instructions

1. In a medium saucepan, combine the heavy cream, whole milk, and sugar. Heat over medium heat, stirring occasionally, until the sugar is fully dissolved and the mixture is hot but not boiling. Remove from heat.

2. In a mixing bowl, whisk the egg yolks until pale and creamy. Slowly add 1/2 cup of the warm cream mixture to the yolks, whisking constantly to temper them.

3. Gradually whisk the tempered yolks back into the saucepan with the remaining cream mixture.

4. Return the saucepan to medium-low heat and cook, stirring constantly, until the custard thickens and coats the back of a spoon (170–175°F). Do not let it boil.

5. Strain the custard through a fine-mesh sieve into a clean bowl to remove any lumps. Stir in the lemon curd and vanilla extract until smooth and well mixed.

6. Allow the custard to cool to room temperature, then cover and refrigerate for at least 4 hours or overnight until thoroughly chilled.

7. Freeze your KitchenAid Ice Cream Maker bowl for 24 hours. Assemble the attachment, attach the dasher, and turn the stand mixer to "Stir" speed.

8. Pour the chilled custard into the frozen bowl and churn for 20–25 minutes until the ice cream reaches a soft-serve consistency.

9. During the last 5 minutes of churning, gradually add the crushed graham crackers and mini marshmallows or meringue pieces, ensuring they are evenly distributed.

10. Transfer the ice cream to an airtight container and freeze for 2–3 hours for a firmer texture before serving.

Nutritional Information (Per Serving)

- Calories: 340 | Carbohydrates: 30g
- Protein Content: 5g | Total Fiber: 1g | Fats: 23g

Birthday Cake Blast Ice Cream

Time Needed to Prepare: 30 minutes (plus chilling time)
KitchenAid Time: 20–25 minutes
Servings: 8

Ingredients List

- 2 cups of heavy cream
- 1 cup of whole milk
- 3/4 cup of granulated sugar
- 4 large egg yolks
- 1 teaspoon pure vanilla extract
- 1 teaspoon pure almond extract
- 1 cup of crumbled yellow cake (store-bought or homemade)
- 1/2 cup of rainbow sprinkles

Instructions

1. In a medium saucepan, combine the heavy cream, whole milk, and sugar. Heat over medium heat, stirring occasionally, until the sugar is fully dissolved and the mixture is hot but not boiling. Remove from heat.
2. In a mixing bowl, whisk the egg yolks until pale and creamy. Slowly add 1/2 cup of the warm cream mixture to the yolks, whisking constantly to temper them.
3. Gradually whisk the tempered yolks back into the saucepan with the remaining cream mixture.
4. Return the saucepan to medium-low heat and cook, stirring constantly, until the custard thickens and coats the back of a spoon (170–175°F). Do not let it boil.
5. Strain the custard through a fine-mesh sieve into a clean bowl to remove any lumps. Stir in the vanilla extract and almond extract.
6. Allow the custard to cool to room temperature, then cover and refrigerate for at least 4 hours or overnight until thoroughly chilled.
7. Freeze your KitchenAid Ice Cream Maker bowl for 24 hours. Assemble the attachment, attach the dasher, and turn the stand mixer to "Stir" speed.
8. Pour the chilled custard into the frozen bowl and churn for 20–25 minutes until the ice cream reaches a soft-serve consistency.
9. During the last 5 minutes of churning, gradually add the crumbled yellow cake and rainbow sprinkles, ensuring they are evenly distributed.
10. Transfer the ice cream to an airtight container and freeze for 2–3 hours for a firmer texture before serving.

Nutritional Information (Per Serving)

- Calories: 350 | Carbohydrates: 32g
- Protein Content: 5g | Total Fiber: 0g | Fats: 24g

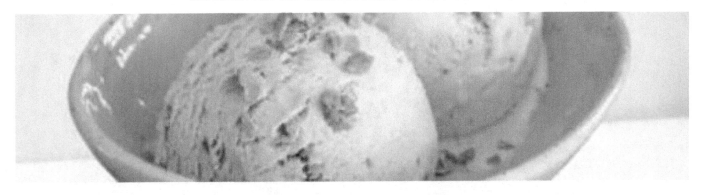

Maple Walnut Ice Cream

Time Needed to Prepare: 30 minutes (plus chilling time)
KitchenAid Time: 20–25 minutes
Servings: 8

Ingredients List

- 2 cups of heavy cream
- 1 cup of whole milk
- 3/4 cup of pure maple syrup
- 4 large egg yolks
- 1 teaspoon pure vanilla extract
- 1 cup of chopped walnuts, toasted

Instructions

1. In a medium saucepan, combine the heavy cream, whole milk, and maple syrup. Heat over medium heat, stirring occasionally, until the mixture is hot but not boiling. Remove from heat.

2. In a mixing bowl, whisk the egg yolks until pale and creamy. Slowly add 1/2 cup of the warm cream mixture to the yolks, whisking constantly to temper them.

3. Gradually whisk the tempered yolks back into the saucepan with the remaining cream mixture.

4. Return the saucepan to medium-low heat and cook, stirring constantly, until the custard thickens and coats the back of a spoon (170–175°F). Do not let it boil.

5. Strain the custard through a fine-mesh sieve into a clean bowl to remove any lumps. Stir in the vanilla extract.

6. Allow the custard to cool to room temperature, then cover and refrigerate for at least 4 hours or overnight until thoroughly chilled.

7. Freeze your KitchenAid Ice Cream Maker bowl for 24 hours. Assemble the attachment, attach the dasher, and turn the stand mixer to "Stir" speed.

8. Pour the chilled custard into the frozen bowl and churn for 20–25 minutes until the ice cream reaches a soft-serve consistency.

9. During the last 5 minutes of churning, gradually add the toasted walnuts, ensuring they are evenly distributed.

10. Transfer the ice cream to an airtight container and freeze for 2–3 hours for a firmer texture before serving.

Nutritional Information (Per Serving)

- Calories: 320 | Carbohydrates: 27g
- Protein Content: 5g | Total Fiber: 1g | Fats: 23g

Rocky Road Ice Cream

Time Needed to Prepare: 30 minutes (plus chilling time)
KitchenAid Time: 20–25 minutes
Servings: 8

Ingredients List

- 2 cups of heavy cream
- 1 cup of whole milk
- 3/4 cup of granulated sugar
- 4 large egg yolks
- 1/2 cup of unsweetened cocoa powder
- 1 teaspoon pure vanilla extract
- 1 cup of mini marshmallows
- 1/2 cup of chopped almonds, toasted
- 1/2 cup of semisweet chocolate chunks

Instructions

1. In a medium saucepan, combine the heavy cream, whole milk, sugar, and cocoa powder. Heat over medium heat, whisking occasionally, until the sugar is fully dissolved, and the mixture is hot but not boiling. Remove from heat.
2. In a mixing bowl, whisk the egg yolks until pale and creamy. Slowly add 1/2 cup of the warm cocoa mixture to the yolks, whisking constantly to temper them.
3. Gradually whisk the tempered yolks back into the saucepan with the remaining cocoa mixture.
4. Return the saucepan to medium-low heat and cook, stirring constantly, until the custard thickens and coats the back of a spoon (170–175°F). Do not let it boil.
5. Strain the custard through a fine-mesh sieve into a clean bowl to remove any lumps. Stir in the vanilla extract.
6. Allow the custard to cool to room temperature, then cover and refrigerate for at least 4 hours or overnight until thoroughly chilled.
7. Freeze your KitchenAid Ice Cream Maker bowl for 24 hours. Assemble the attachment, attach the dasher, and turn the stand mixer to "Stir" speed.
8. Pour the chilled custard into the frozen bowl and churn for 20–25 minutes until the ice cream reaches a soft-serve consistency.
9. During the last 5 minutes of churning, gradually add the mini marshmallows, toasted almonds, and chocolate chunks, ensuring they are evenly distributed.
10. Transfer the ice cream to an airtight container and freeze for 2–3 hours for a firmer texture before serving.

Nutritional Information (Per Serving)

- Calories: 350 | Carbohydrates: 30g
- Protein Content: 6g | Total Fiber: 2g | Fats: 25g

Coconut Cream Ice Cream

Time Needed to Prepare: 30 minutes (plus chilling time)
KitchenAid Time: 20–25 minutes
Servings: 8

Ingredients List

- 2 cups of coconut milk (full-fat)
- 1 cup of heavy cream
- 3/4 cup of granulated sugar
- 4 large egg yolks
- 1 teaspoon pure vanilla extract
- 1/2 cup of shredded sweetened coconut, toasted

Instructions

1. In a medium saucepan, combine the coconut milk, heavy cream, and sugar. Heat over medium heat, stirring occasionally, until the sugar is fully dissolved and the mixture is hot but not boiling. Remove from heat.

2. In a mixing bowl, whisk the egg yolks until pale and creamy. Slowly add 1/2 cup of the warm coconut mixture to the yolks, whisking constantly to temper them.

3. Gradually whisk the tempered yolks back into the saucepan with the remaining coconut mixture.

4. Return the saucepan to medium-low heat and cook, stirring constantly, until the custard thickens and coats the back of a spoon (170–175°F). Do not let it boil.

5. Strain the custard through a fine-mesh sieve into a clean bowl to remove any lumps. Stir in the vanilla extract.

6. Allow the custard to cool to room temperature, then cover and refrigerate for at least 4 hours or overnight until thoroughly chilled.

7. Freeze your KitchenAid Ice Cream Maker bowl for 24 hours. Assemble the attachment, attach the dasher, and turn the stand mixer to "Stir" speed.

8. Pour the chilled custard into the frozen bowl and churn for 20–25 minutes until the ice cream reaches a soft-serve consistency.

9. During the last 5 minutes of churning, gradually add the toasted shredded coconut, ensuring it is evenly distributed.

10. Transfer the ice cream to an airtight container and freeze for 2–3 hours for a firmer texture before serving.

Nutritional Information (Per Serving)

- Calories: 310　|　Carbohydrates: 25g
- Protein Content: 4g　|　Total Fiber: 1g　|　Fats: 23g

21

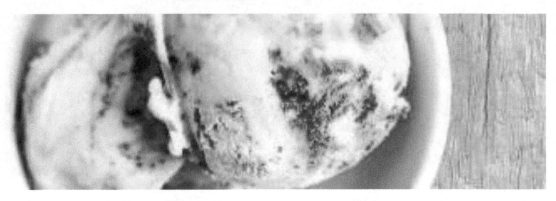

Black Raspberry Ripple Ice Cream

Time Needed to Prepare: 35 minutes (plus chilling time)
KitchenAid Time: 20–25 minutes
Servings: 8

Ingredients List

- 2 cups of heavy cream
- 1 cup of whole milk
- 3/4 cup of granulated sugar
- 4 large egg yolks
- 1 teaspoon pure vanilla extract
- 1 1/2 cups of fresh black raspberries (or frozen, thawed)
- 1/4 cup of granulated sugar (for the raspberry ripple)
- 1 tablespoon of lemon juice

Instructions

1. In a medium saucepan, combine the heavy cream, whole milk, and sugar. Heat over medium heat, stirring occasionally, until the sugar is fully dissolved and the mixture is hot but not boiling. Remove from heat.

2. In a mixing bowl, whisk the egg yolks until pale and creamy. Slowly add 1/2 cup of the warm cream mixture to the yolks, whisking constantly to temper them.

3. Gradually whisk the tempered yolks back into the saucepan with the remaining cream mixture.

4. Return the saucepan to medium-low heat and cook, stirring constantly, until the custard thickens and coats the back of a spoon (170–175°F). Do not let it boil.

5. Strain the custard through a fine-mesh sieve into a clean bowl to remove any lumps. Stir in the vanilla extract.

6. Allow the custard to cool to room temperature, then cover and refrigerate for at least 4 hours or overnight until thoroughly chilled.

7. In a small saucepan, combine the black raspberries, 1/4 cup of sugar, and lemon juice. Cook over medium heat, stirring occasionally, until the berries break down and form a syrupy mixture (about 10 minutes). Strain the mixture through a fine-mesh sieve to remove seeds, and let it cool completely.

8. Freeze your KitchenAid Ice Cream Maker bowl for 24 hours. Assemble the attachment, attach the dasher, and turn the stand mixer to "Stir" speed.

9. Pour the chilled custard into the frozen bowl and churn for 20–25 minutes until the ice cream reaches a soft-serve consistency.

10. Spoon half of the churned ice cream into an airtight container, drizzle with half of the raspberry syrup, and gently swirl with a knife. Repeat with the remaining ice cream and syrup.

11. Freeze the ice cream for 2–3 hours for a firmer texture before serving.

Nutritional Information (Per Serving)

- Calories: 310 | Carbohydrates: 27g
- Protein Content: 5g | Total Fiber: 1g | Fats: 22g

Honey Lavender Ice Cream

Time Needed to Prepare: 40 minutes (plus chilling time)
KitchenAid Time: 20–25 minutes
Servings: 8

Ingredients List

- 2 cups of heavy cream
- 1 cup of whole milk
- 1/2 cup of honey
- 4 large egg yolks
- 2 tablespoons of dried culinary lavender
- 1 teaspoon pure vanilla extract

Instructions

1. In a medium saucepan, combine the heavy cream, whole milk, and honey. Heat over medium heat, stirring occasionally, until the honey is fully dissolved and the mixture is hot but not boiling. Remove from heat.

2. Add the dried lavender to the hot mixture, cover, and steep for 15 minutes. Strain the mixture through a fine-mesh sieve into a clean saucepan to remove the lavender.

3. In a mixing bowl, whisk the egg yolks until pale and creamy. Slowly add 1/2 cup of the warm cream mixture to the yolks, whisking constantly to temper them.

4. Gradually whisk the tempered yolks back into the saucepan with the remaining cream mixture.

5. Return the saucepan to medium-low heat and cook, stirring constantly, until the custard thickens and coats the back of a spoon (170–175°F). Do not let it boil.

6. Strain the custard through a fine-mesh sieve into a clean bowl to remove any lumps. Stir in the vanilla extract.

7. Allow the custard to cool to room temperature, then cover and refrigerate for at least 4 hours or overnight until thoroughly chilled.

8. Freeze your KitchenAid Ice Cream Maker bowl for 24 hours. Assemble the attachment, attach the dasher, and turn the stand mixer to "Stir" speed.

9. Pour the chilled custard into the frozen bowl and churn for 20–25 minutes until the ice cream reaches a soft-serve consistency.

10. Transfer the ice cream to an airtight container and freeze for 2–3 hours for a firmer texture before serving.

Nutritional Information (Per Serving)

- Calories: 290 | Carbohydrates: 25g
- Protein Content: 4g | Total Fiber: 0g | Fats: 22g

Churro Cinnamon Ice Cream

Time Needed to Prepare: 35 minutes (plus chilling time)
KitchenAid Time: 20–25 minutes
Servings: 8

Ingredients List

- 2 cups of heavy cream
- 1 cup of whole milk
- 3/4 cup of granulated sugar
- 4 large egg yolks
- 1 teaspoon pure vanilla extract
- 2 teaspoons ground cinnamon
- 1/2 cup of crushed churros or cinnamon sugar-coated cookies

Instructions

1. In a medium saucepan, combine the heavy cream, whole milk, sugar, and ground cinnamon. Heat over medium heat, stirring occasionally, until the sugar is fully dissolved and the mixture is hot but not boiling. Remove from heat.

2. In a mixing bowl, whisk the egg yolks until pale and creamy. Slowly add 1/2 cup of the warm cream mixture to the yolks, whisking constantly to temper them.

3. Gradually whisk the tempered yolks back into the saucepan with the remaining cream mixture.

4. Return the saucepan to medium-low heat and cook, stirring constantly, until the custard thickens and coats the back of a spoon (170–175°F). Do not let it boil.

5. Strain the custard through a fine-mesh sieve into a clean bowl to remove any lumps. Stir in the vanilla extract.

6. Allow the custard to cool to room temperature, then cover and refrigerate for at least 4 hours or overnight until thoroughly chilled.

7. Freeze your KitchenAid Ice Cream Maker bowl for 24 hours. Assemble the attachment, attach the dasher, and turn the stand mixer to "Stir" speed.

8. Pour the chilled custard into the frozen bowl and churn for 20–25 minutes until the ice cream reaches a soft-serve consistency.

9. During the last 5 minutes of churning, gradually add the crushed churros or cinnamon sugar-coated cookies, ensuring they are evenly distributed.

10. Transfer the ice cream to an airtight container and freeze for 2–3 hours for a firmer texture before serving.

Nutritional Information (Per Serving)

- Calories: 320 | Carbohydrates: 28g
- Protein Content: 5g | Total Fiber: 1g | Fats: 23g

Butter Pecan Ice Cream

Time Needed to Prepare: 35 minutes (plus chilling time)
KitchenAid Time: 20–25 minutes
Servings: 8

Ingredients List

- 2 cups of heavy cream
- 1 cup of whole milk
- 3/4 cup of granulated sugar
- 4 large egg yolks
- 1 teaspoon pure vanilla extract
- 1/4 cup of salted butter
- 1 cup of chopped pecans, toasted

Instructions

1. In a medium skillet, melt the butter over medium heat. Add the chopped pecans and cook, stirring frequently, for 4–5 minutes until fragrant and lightly toasted. Remove from heat and set aside to cool.

2. In a medium saucepan, combine the heavy cream, whole milk, and sugar. Heat over medium heat, stirring occasionally, until the sugar is fully dissolved and the mixture is hot but not boiling. Remove from heat.

3. In a mixing bowl, whisk the egg yolks until pale and creamy. Slowly add 1/2 cup of the warm cream mixture to the yolks, whisking constantly to temper them.

4. Gradually whisk the tempered yolks back into the saucepan with the remaining cream mixture.

5. Return the saucepan to medium-low heat and cook, stirring constantly, until the custard thickens and coats the back of a spoon (170–175°F). Do not let it boil.

6. Strain the custard through a fine-mesh sieve into a clean bowl to remove any lumps. Stir in the vanilla extract.

7. Allow the custard to cool to room temperature, then cover and refrigerate for at least 4 hours or overnight until thoroughly chilled.

8. Freeze your KitchenAid Ice Cream Maker bowl for 24 hours. Assemble the attachment, attach the dasher, and turn the stand mixer to "Stir" speed.

9. Pour the chilled custard into the frozen bowl and churn for 20–25 minutes until the ice cream reaches a soft-serve consistency.

10. During the last 5 minutes of churning, gradually add the toasted pecans, ensuring they are evenly distributed.

11. Transfer the ice cream to an airtight container and freeze for 2–3 hours for a firmer texture before serving.

Nutritional Information (Per Serving)

- Calories: 330 | Carbohydrates: 26g
- Protein Content: 5g | Total Fiber: 1g | Fats: 25g

CHAPTER 2: GELATOS

Italian Pistachio Gelato

Time Needed to Prepare: 40 minutes (plus chilling time)
KitchenAid Time: 20–25 minutes
Servings: 6

Ingredients List

- 2 cups of whole milk
- 1 cup of heavy cream
- 3/4 cup of granulated sugar
- 4 large egg yolks
- 1/2 cup of pistachio paste
- 1/2 teaspoon pure almond extract
- 1/2 teaspoon pure vanilla extract
- 1/4 cup of finely chopped pistachios (optional, for garnish)

Instructions

1. In a medium saucepan, combine the whole milk, heavy cream, and sugar. Heat over medium heat, stirring occasionally, until the sugar is fully dissolved and the mixture is hot but not boiling. Remove from heat.
2. In a mixing bowl, whisk the egg yolks until pale and creamy. Slowly add 1/2 cup of the warm milk mixture to the yolks, whisking constantly to temper them.
3. Gradually whisk the tempered yolks back into the saucepan with the remaining milk mixture.
4. Return the saucepan to medium-low heat and cook, stirring constantly, until the custard thickens and coats the back of a spoon (170–175°F). Do not let it boil.
5. Remove from heat and strain the custard through a fine-mesh sieve into a clean bowl to remove any lumps. Stir in the pistachio paste, almond extract, and vanilla extract until fully incorporated.
6. Allow the custard to cool to room temperature, then cover and refrigerate for at least 4 hours or overnight until thoroughly chilled.
7. Freeze your KitchenAid Ice Cream Maker bowl for 24 hours. Assemble the attachment, attach the dasher, and turn the stand mixer to "Stir" speed.
8. Pour the chilled custard into the frozen bowl and churn for 20–25 minutes until the gelato reaches a soft-serve consistency.
9. Transfer the gelato to an airtight container, garnish with finely chopped pistachios (if desired), and freeze for 2–3 hours for a firmer texture before serving.

Nutritional Information (Per Serving)

- Calories: 290 | Carbohydrates: 25g

- Protein Content: 6g | Total Fiber: 1g | Fats: 20g

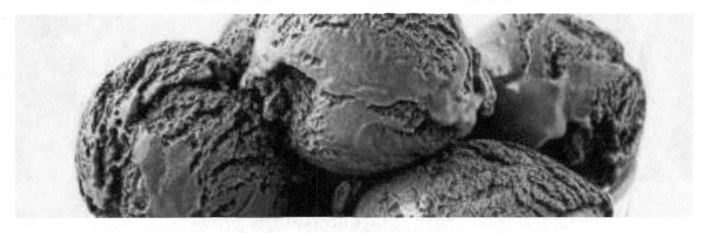

Dark Chocolate Espresso Gelato

Time Needed to Prepare: 40 minutes (plus chilling time)
KitchenAid Time: 20–25 minutes
Servings: 6

Ingredients List

- 2 cups of whole milk
- 1 cup of heavy cream
- 3/4 cup of granulated sugar
- 4 large egg yolks
- 1/2 cup of dark chocolate, finely chopped
- 2 tablespoons of unsweetened cocoa powder
- 1 tablespoon of instant espresso powder
- 1 teaspoon pure vanilla extract

Instructions

1. In a medium saucepan, combine the whole milk, heavy cream, and sugar. Heat over medium heat, stirring occasionally, until the sugar is fully dissolved and the mixture is hot but not boiling. Remove from heat.
2. Whisk the cocoa powder and instant espresso powder into the warm milk mixture until fully dissolved.
3. In a mixing bowl, whisk the egg yolks until pale and creamy. Slowly add 1/2 cup of the warm milk mixture to the yolks, whisking constantly to temper them.
4. Gradually whisk the tempered yolks back into the saucepan with the remaining milk mixture.
5. Return the saucepan to medium-low heat and cook, stirring constantly, until the custard thickens and coats the back of a spoon (170–175°F). Do not let it boil.
6. Remove from heat and stir in the chopped dark chocolate until completely melted and smooth. Strain the custard through a fine-mesh sieve into a clean bowl to remove any lumps. Stir in the vanilla extract.
7. Allow the custard to cool to room temperature, then cover and refrigerate for at least 4 hours or overnight until thoroughly chilled.
8. Freeze your KitchenAid Ice Cream Maker bowl for 24 hours. Assemble the attachment, attach the dasher, and turn the stand mixer to "Stir" speed.
9. Pour the chilled custard into the frozen bowl and churn for 20–25 minutes until the gelato reaches a soft-serve consistency.
10. Transfer the gelato to an airtight container and freeze for 2–3 hours for a firmer texture before serving.

Nutritional Information (Per Serving)

- Calories: 300 | Carbohydrates: 28g
- Protein Content: 6g | Total Fiber: 2g | Fats: 21g

Stracciatella Gelato

Time Needed to Prepare: 35 minutes (plus chilling time)
KitchenAid Time: 20–25 minutes
Servings: 6

Ingredients List

- 2 cups of whole milk

- 1 cup of heavy cream

- 3/4 cup of granulated sugar

- 4 large egg yolks

- 1 teaspoon pure vanilla extract

- 1/2 cup of dark chocolate, finely chopped or melted

Instructions

1. In a medium saucepan, combine the whole milk, heavy cream, and sugar. Heat over medium heat, stirring occasionally, until the sugar is fully dissolved and the mixture is hot but not boiling. Remove from heat.

2. In a mixing bowl, whisk the egg yolks until pale and creamy. Slowly add 1/2 cup of the warm milk mixture to the yolks, whisking constantly to temper them.

3. Gradually whisk the tempered yolks back into the saucepan with the remaining milk mixture.

4. Return the saucepan to medium-low heat and cook, stirring constantly, until the custard thickens and coats the back of a spoon (170–175°F). Do not let it boil.

5. Strain the custard through a fine-mesh sieve into a clean bowl to remove any lumps. Stir in the vanilla extract.

6. Allow the custard to cool to room temperature, then cover and refrigerate for at least 4 hours or overnight until thoroughly chilled.

7. Freeze your KitchenAid Ice Cream Maker bowl for 24 hours. Assemble the attachment, attach the dasher, and turn the stand mixer to "Stir" speed.

8. Pour the chilled custard into the frozen bowl and churn for 20–25 minutes until the gelato reaches a soft-serve consistency.

9. During the last few minutes of churning, drizzle the melted dark chocolate into the gelato in a thin stream while it continues to churn. This will create delicate chocolate flakes (stracciatella).

10. Transfer the gelato to an airtight container and freeze for 2–3 hours for a firmer texture before serving.

Nutritional Information (Per Serving)

- Calories: 290 | Carbohydrates: 26g

- Protein Content: 6g | Total Fiber: 1g | Fats: 20g

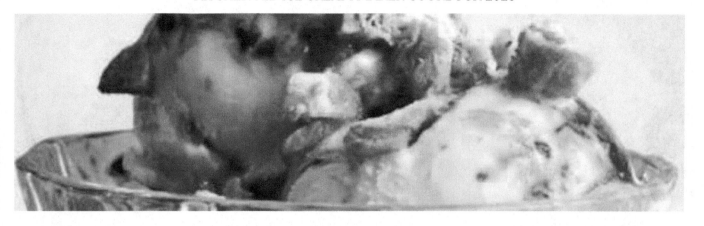

Hazelnut Heaven Gelato

Time Needed to Prepare: 40 minutes (plus chilling time)
KitchenAid Time: 20–25 minutes
Servings: 6

Ingredients List

- 2 cups of whole milk
- 1 cup of heavy cream
- 3/4 cup of granulated sugar
- 4 large egg yolks
- 1/2 cup of hazelnut paste
- 1/2 teaspoon pure vanilla extract
- 1/4 cup of toasted hazelnuts, chopped

Instructions

1. In a medium saucepan, combine the whole milk, heavy cream, and sugar. Heat over medium heat, stirring occasionally, until the sugar is fully dissolved and the mixture is hot but not boiling. Remove from heat.

2. In a mixing bowl, whisk the egg yolks until pale and creamy. Slowly add 1/2 cup of the warm milk mixture to the yolks, whisking constantly to temper them.

3. Gradually whisk the tempered yolks back into the saucepan with the remaining milk mixture.

4. Return the saucepan to medium-low heat and cook, stirring constantly, until the custard thickens and coats the back of a spoon (170–175°F). Do not let it boil.

5. Remove from heat and stir in the hazelnut paste until fully incorporated. Strain the custard through a fine-mesh sieve into a clean bowl to remove any lumps. Stir in the vanilla extract.

6. Allow the custard to cool to room temperature, then cover and refrigerate for at least 4 hours or overnight until thoroughly chilled.

7. Freeze your KitchenAid Ice Cream Maker bowl for 24 hours. Assemble the attachment, attach the dasher, and turn the stand mixer to "Stir" speed.

8. Pour the chilled custard into the frozen bowl and churn for 20–25 minutes until the gelato reaches a soft-serve consistency.

9. During the last 5 minutes of churning, gradually add the toasted hazelnuts, ensuring they are evenly distributed.

10. Transfer the gelato to an airtight container and freeze for 2–3 hours for a firmer texture before serving.

Nutritional Information (Per Serving)

- Calories: 320 | Carbohydrates: 25g
- Protein Content: 7g | Total Fiber: 2g | Fats: 23g

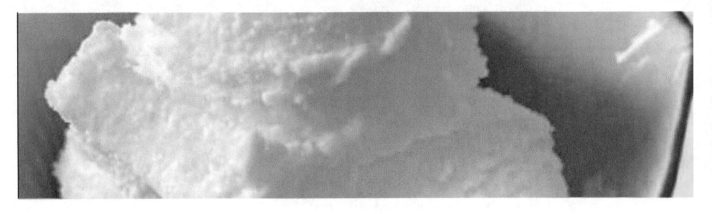

Lemon Zest Gelato

Time Needed to Prepare: 35 minutes (plus chilling time)
KitchenAid Time: 20–25 minutes
Servings: 6

Ingredients List

- 2 cups of whole milk
- 1 cup of heavy cream
- 3/4 cup of granulated sugar
- 4 large egg yolks
- Zest of 2 lemons
- 1/4 cup of fresh lemon juice
- 1/2 teaspoon pure vanilla extract

Instructions

1. In a medium saucepan, combine the whole milk, heavy cream, and sugar. Heat over medium heat, stirring occasionally, until the sugar is fully dissolved and the mixture is hot but not boiling. Remove from heat.

2. Stir in the lemon zest and let steep for 15 minutes. Strain the mixture through a fine-mesh sieve to remove the zest.

3. In a mixing bowl, whisk the egg yolks until pale and creamy. Slowly add 1/2 cup of the warm milk mixture to the yolks, whisking constantly to temper them.

4. Gradually whisk the tempered yolks back into the saucepan with the remaining milk mixture.

5. Return the saucepan to medium-low heat and cook, stirring constantly, until the custard thickens and coats the back of a spoon (170–175°F). Do not let it boil.

6. Remove from heat and stir in the fresh lemon juice and vanilla extract. Strain the custard through a fine-mesh sieve into a clean bowl to remove any lumps.

7. Allow the custard to cool to room temperature, then cover and refrigerate for at least 4 hours or overnight until thoroughly chilled.

8. Freeze your KitchenAid Ice Cream Maker bowl for 24 hours. Assemble the attachment, attach the dasher, and turn the stand mixer to "Stir" speed.

9. Pour the chilled custard into the frozen bowl and churn for 20–25 minutes until the gelato reaches a soft-serve consistency.

10. Transfer the gelato to an airtight container and freeze for 2–3 hours for a firmer texture before serving.

Nutritional Information (Per Serving)

- Calories: 280 | Carbohydrates: 26g

- Protein Content: 6g | Total Fiber: 0g | Fats: 18g

Vanilla Fior di Latte Gelato

Time Needed to Prepare: 30 minutes (plus chilling time)
KitchenAid Time: 20–25 minutes
Servings: 6

Ingredients List

- 2 cups of whole milk

- 1 cup of heavy cream

- 3/4 cup of granulated sugar

- 1 teaspoon pure vanilla extract

Instructions

1. In a medium saucepan, combine the whole milk, heavy cream, and sugar. Heat over medium heat, stirring occasionally, until the sugar is fully dissolved and the mixture is hot but not boiling. Remove from heat.

2. Gradually whisk the milk mixture into the saucepan.

3. Return the saucepan to medium-low heat and cook, stirring constantly, until the custard thickens and coats the back of a spoon (170–175°F). Do not let it boil.

4. Strain the custard through a fine-mesh sieve into a clean bowl to remove any lumps. Stir in the vanilla extract.

5. Allow the custard to cool to room temperature, then cover and refrigerate for at least 4 hours or overnight until thoroughly chilled.

6. Freeze your KitchenAid Ice Cream Maker bowl for 24 hours. Assemble the attachment, attach the dasher, and turn the stand mixer to "Stir" speed.

7. Pour the chilled custard into the frozen bowl and churn for 20–25 minutes until the gelato reaches a soft-serve consistency.

8. Transfer the gelato to an airtight container and freeze for 2–3 hours for a firmer texture before serving.

Nutritional Information (Per Serving)

- Calories: 260

- Carbohydrates: 25g

- Protein Content: 6g

- Total Fiber: 0g

- Fats: 16g

Blood Orange Gelato

Time Needed to Prepare: 35 minutes (plus chilling time)
KitchenAid Time: 20–25 minutes
Servings: 6

Ingredients List

- 2 cups of whole milk
- 1 cup of heavy cream
- 3/4 cup of granulated sugar
- 4 large egg yolks
- 1/2 cup of fresh blood orange juice
- Zest of 1 blood orange
- 1/2 teaspoon pure vanilla extract

Instructions

1. In a medium saucepan, combine the whole milk, heavy cream, and sugar. Heat over medium heat, stirring occasionally, until the sugar is fully dissolved and the mixture is hot but not boiling. Remove from heat.

2. In a mixing bowl, whisk the egg yolks until pale and creamy. Slowly add 1/2 cup of the warm milk mixture to the yolks, whisking constantly to temper them.

3. Gradually whisk the tempered yolks back into the saucepan with the remaining milk mixture.

4. Return the saucepan to medium-low heat and cook, stirring constantly, until the custard thickens and coats the back of a spoon (170–175°F). Do not let it boil.

5. Remove from heat and stir in the blood orange juice and zest. Strain the custard through a fine-mesh sieve into a clean bowl to remove any lumps. Stir in the vanilla extract.

6. Allow the custard to cool to room temperature, then cover and refrigerate for at least 4 hours or overnight until thoroughly chilled.

7. Freeze your KitchenAid Ice Cream Maker bowl for 24 hours. Assemble the attachment, attach the dasher, and turn the stand mixer to "Stir" speed.

8. Pour the chilled custard into the frozen bowl and churn for 20–25 minutes until the gelato reaches a soft-serve consistency.

9. Transfer the gelato to an airtight container and freeze for 2–3 hours for a firmer texture before serving.

Nutritional Information (Per Serving)

- Calories: 280
- Carbohydrates: 27g
- Protein Content: 6g
- Total Fiber: 0g
- Fats: 18g

Tiramisu Delight Gelato

Time Needed to Prepare: 40 minutes (plus chilling time)
KitchenAid Time: 20–25 minutes
Servings: 6

Ingredients List

- 2 cups of whole milk
- 1 cup of heavy cream
- 3/4 cup of granulated sugar
- 4 large egg yolks
- 1 tablespoon of instant espresso powder
- 1/4 cup of mascarpone cheese
- 1 teaspoon pure vanilla extract
- 1/2 cup of crushed ladyfinger cookies
- 2 tablespoons of cocoa powder (for garnish)

Instructions

1. In a medium saucepan, combine the whole milk, heavy cream, and sugar. Heat over medium heat, stirring occasionally, until the sugar is fully dissolved and the mixture is hot but not boiling. Remove from heat.
2. Dissolve the instant espresso powder in the warm milk mixture.
3. In a mixing bowl, whisk the egg yolks until pale and creamy. Slowly add 1/2 cup of the warm milk mixture to the yolks, whisking constantly to temper them.
4. Gradually whisk the tempered yolks back into the saucepan with the remaining milk mixture.
5. Return the saucepan to medium-low heat and cook, stirring constantly, until the custard thickens and coats the back of a spoon (170–175°F). Do not let it boil.
6. Remove from heat and strain the custard through a fine-mesh sieve into a clean bowl to remove any lumps. Stir in the mascarpone cheese until fully incorporated, then add the vanilla extract.
7. Allow the custard to cool to room temperature, then cover and refrigerate for at least 4 hours or overnight until thoroughly chilled.
8. Freeze your KitchenAid Ice Cream Maker bowl for 24 hours. Assemble the attachment, attach the dasher, and turn the stand mixer to "Stir" speed.
9. Pour the chilled custard into the frozen bowl and churn for 20–25 minutes until the gelato reaches a soft-serve consistency.
10. During the last 5 minutes of churning, gradually add the crushed ladyfinger cookies, ensuring they are evenly distributed.
11. Transfer the gelato to an airtight container and freeze for 2–3 hours for a firmer texture. Garnish with a light dusting of cocoa powder before serving.

Nutritional Information (Per Serving)

- Calories: 330 | Carbohydrates: 29g
- Protein Content: 6g | Total Fiber: 1g | Fats: 22g

Salted Almond Gelato

Time Needed to Prepare: 40 minutes (plus chilling time)
KitchenAid Time: 20–25 minutes
Servings: 6

Ingredients List

- 2 cups of whole milk
- 1 cup of heavy cream
- 3/4 cup of granulated sugar
- 4 large egg yolks
- 1/2 teaspoon pure almond extract
- 1 teaspoon pure vanilla extract
- 1/2 cup of roasted salted almonds, finely chopped

Instructions

1. In a medium saucepan, combine the whole milk, heavy cream, and sugar. Heat over medium heat, stirring occasionally, until the sugar is fully dissolved and the mixture is hot but not boiling. Remove from heat.

2. In a mixing bowl, whisk the egg yolks until pale and creamy. Slowly add 1/2 cup of the warm milk mixture to the yolks, whisking constantly to temper them.

3. Gradually whisk the tempered yolks back into the saucepan with the remaining milk mixture.

4. Return the saucepan to medium-low heat and cook, stirring constantly, until the custard thickens and coats the back of a spoon (170–175°F). Do not let it boil.

5. Remove from heat and strain the custard through a fine-mesh sieve into a clean bowl to remove any lumps. Stir in the almond extract and vanilla extract.

6. Allow the custard to cool to room temperature, then cover and refrigerate for at least 4 hours or overnight until thoroughly chilled.

7. Freeze your KitchenAid Ice Cream Maker bowl for 24 hours. Assemble the attachment, attach the dasher, and turn the stand mixer to "Stir" speed.

8. Pour the chilled custard into the frozen bowl and churn for 20–25 minutes until the gelato reaches a soft-serve consistency.

9. During the last 5 minutes of churning, gradually add the chopped roasted salted almonds, ensuring they are evenly distributed.

10. Transfer the gelato to an airtight container and freeze for 2–3 hours for a firmer texture before serving.

Nutritional Information (Per Serving)

- Calories: 310 | Carbohydrates: 26g

- Protein Content: 6g | Total Fiber: 1g | Fats: 20g

Wild Berry Gelato

Time Needed to Prepare: 40 minutes (plus chilling time)
KitchenAid Time: 20–25 minutes
Servings: 6

Ingredients List

- 2 cups of whole milk
- 1 cup of heavy cream
- 3/4 cup of granulated sugar
- 4 large egg yolks
- 1 cup of mixed wild berries (blueberries, blackberries, raspberries, or strawberries)
- 1/4 cup of granulated sugar (for the berry sauce)
- 1 tablespoon of lemon juice
- 1/2 teaspoon pure vanilla extract

Instructions

1. In a small saucepan, combine the wild berries, 1/4 cup of sugar, and lemon juice. Cook over medium heat, stirring occasionally, until the berries break down and form a thick sauce (about 10 minutes). Strain the mixture through a fine-mesh sieve to remove seeds and let it cool completely.

2. In a medium saucepan, combine the whole milk, heavy cream, and 3/4 cup of sugar. Heat over medium heat, stirring occasionally, until the sugar is fully dissolved and the mixture is hot but not boiling. Remove from heat.

3. In a mixing bowl, whisk the egg yolks until pale and creamy. Slowly add 1/2 cup of the warm milk mixture to the yolks, whisking constantly to temper them.

4. Gradually whisk the tempered yolks back into the saucepan with the remaining milk mixture.

5. Return the saucepan to medium-low heat and cook, stirring constantly, until the custard thickens and coats the back of a spoon (170–175°F). Do not let it boil.

6. Remove from heat and strain the custard through a fine-mesh sieve into a clean bowl to remove any lumps. Stir in the vanilla extract and half of the berry sauce.

7. Allow the custard to cool to room temperature, then cover and refrigerate for at least 4 hours or overnight until thoroughly chilled.

8. Freeze your KitchenAid Ice Cream Maker bowl for 24 hours. Assemble the attachment, attach the dasher, and turn the stand mixer to "Stir" speed.

9. Pour the chilled custard into the frozen bowl and churn for 20–25 minutes until the gelato reaches a soft-serve consistency.

10. Spoon half of the churned gelato into an airtight container, drizzle with the remaining berry sauce, and gently swirl with a knife. Repeat with the remaining gelato and sauce.

11. Freeze the gelato for 2–3 hours for a firmer texture before serving.

Nutritional Information (Per Serving)

- Calories: 290 | Carbohydrates: 28g

- Protein Content: 6g | Total Fiber: 1g | Fats: 18g

CHAPTER 3: SORBETS

Classic Lemon Sorbet

Time Needed to Prepare: 20 minutes (plus chilling time)
KitchenAid Time: 20–25 minutes
Servings: 6

Ingredients List

- 2 cups of water
- 1 cup of granulated sugar
- 1 cup of fresh lemon juice (about 4–5 lemons)
- Zest of 1 lemon

Instructions

1. In a medium saucepan, combine the water and sugar. Heat over medium heat, stirring occasionally, until the sugar is fully dissolved and the mixture comes to a gentle simmer. Remove from heat and let cool to room temperature.

2. Stir in the fresh lemon juice and lemon zest. Cover and refrigerate for at least 4 hours or until thoroughly chilled.

3. Freeze your KitchenAid Ice Cream Maker bowl for 24 hours. Assemble the attachment, attach the dasher, and turn the stand mixer to "Stir" speed.

4. Pour the chilled mixture into the frozen bowl and churn for 20–25 minutes until the sorbet reaches a smooth, scoopable consistency.

5. Transfer the sorbet to an airtight container and freeze for 2–3 hours for a firmer texture before serving.

Nutritional Information (Per Serving)

- Calories: 120
- Carbohydrates: 31g
- Protein Content: 0g
- Total Fiber: 0g
- Fats: 0g

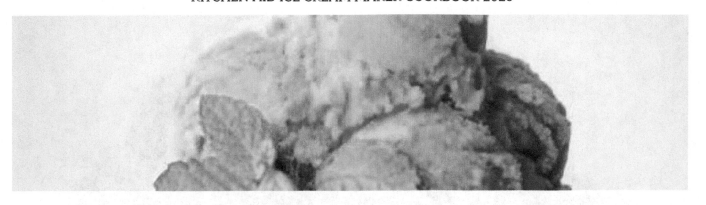

Watermelon Mint Sorbet

Time Needed to Prepare: 25 minutes (plus chilling time)
KitchenAid Time: 20–25 minutes
Servings: 6

Ingredients List

- 4 cups of seedless watermelon, cubed

- 1/2 cup of granulated sugar

- 1/4 cup of water

- 2 tablespoons of fresh mint leaves, finely chopped

- 1 tablespoon of fresh lime juice

Instructions

1. In a small saucepan, combine the sugar and water. Heat over medium heat, stirring occasionally, until the sugar dissolves completely. Remove from heat and let the syrup cool to room temperature.

2. In a blender, puree the watermelon cubes until smooth. Strain the puree through a fine-mesh sieve into a large bowl to remove pulp.

3. Stir the cooled sugar syrup, mint leaves, and lime juice into the watermelon puree. Cover and refrigerate for at least 4 hours or until thoroughly chilled.

4. Freeze your KitchenAid Ice Cream Maker bowl for 24 hours. Assemble the attachment, attach the dasher, and turn the stand mixer to "Stir" speed.

5. Pour the chilled mixture into the frozen bowl and churn for 20–25 minutes until the sorbet reaches a smooth, scoopable consistency.

6. Transfer the sorbet to an airtight container and freeze for 2–3 hours for a firmer texture before serving.

Nutritional Information (Per Serving)

- Calories: 100

- Carbohydrates: 25g

- Protein Content: 1g

- Total Fiber: 1g

- Fats: 0g

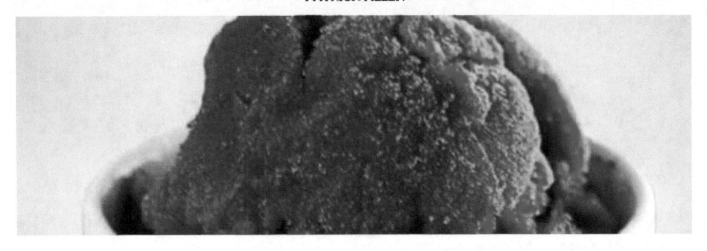

Raspberry Rosé Sorbet

Time Needed to Prepare: 25 minutes (plus chilling time)
KitchenAid Time: 20–25 minutes
Servings: 6

Ingredients List

- 3 cups of fresh raspberries (or frozen, thawed)

- 3/4 cup of granulated sugar

- 1/2 cup of rosé wine

- 1/4 cup of water

- 1 tablespoon of fresh lemon juice

Instructions

1. In a small saucepan, combine the sugar and water. Heat over medium heat, stirring occasionally, until the sugar dissolves completely. Remove from heat and let the syrup cool to room temperature.

2. In a blender, puree the raspberries until smooth. Strain the puree through a fine-mesh sieve into a large bowl to remove seeds.

3. Stir the cooled sugar syrup, rosé wine, and lemon juice into the raspberry puree. Cover and refrigerate for at least 4 hours or until thoroughly chilled.

4. Freeze your KitchenAid Ice Cream Maker bowl for 24 hours. Assemble the attachment, attach the dasher, and turn the stand mixer to "Stir" speed.

5. Pour the chilled mixture into the frozen bowl and churn for 20–25 minutes until the sorbet reaches a smooth, scoopable consistency.

6. Transfer the sorbet to an airtight container and freeze for 2–3 hours for a firmer texture before serving.

Nutritional Information (Per Serving)

- Calories: 110

- Carbohydrates: 24g

- Protein Content: 1g

- Total Fiber: 3g

- Fats: 0g

Pineapple Coconut Sorbet

Time Needed to Prepare: 30 minutes (plus chilling time)
KitchenAid Time: 20–25 minutes
Servings: 6

Ingredients List

- 3 cups of fresh pineapple, cubed (or canned, drained)

- 3/4 cup of coconut milk (full-fat)

- 1/2 cup of granulated sugar

- 1/4 cup of water

- 1 tablespoon of fresh lime juice

Instructions

1. In a small saucepan, combine the sugar and water. Heat over medium heat, stirring occasionally, until the sugar dissolves completely. Remove from heat and let the syrup cool to room temperature.

2. In a blender, puree the pineapple cubes until smooth. Strain the puree through a fine-mesh sieve into a large bowl to remove any pulp.

3. Stir the cooled sugar syrup, coconut milk, and lime juice into the pineapple puree. Cover and refrigerate for at least 4 hours or until thoroughly chilled.

4. Freeze your KitchenAid Ice Cream Maker bowl for 24 hours. Assemble the attachment, attach the dasher, and turn the stand mixer to "Stir" speed.

5. Pour the chilled mixture into the frozen bowl and churn for 20–25 minutes until the sorbet reaches a smooth, scoopable consistency.

6. Transfer the sorbet to an airtight container and freeze for 2–3 hours for a firmer texture before serving.

Nutritional Information (Per Serving)

- Calories: 130

- Carbohydrates: 29g

- Protein Content: 1g

- Total Fiber: 1g

- Fats: 1g

Mango Lime Sorbet

Time Needed to Prepare: 25 minutes (plus chilling time)
KitchenAid Time: 20–25 minutes
Servings: 6

Ingredients List

- 3 cups of ripe mango, peeled and cubed

- 1/2 cup of granulated sugar

- 1/4 cup of water

- 2 tablespoons of fresh lime juice

- Zest of 1 lime

Instructions

1. In a small saucepan, combine the sugar and water. Heat over medium heat, stirring occasionally, until the sugar dissolves completely. Remove from heat and let the syrup cool to room temperature.

2. In a blender, puree the mango until smooth. Strain the puree through a fine-mesh sieve into a large bowl to remove any fibers.

3. Stir the cooled sugar syrup, lime juice, and lime zest into the mango puree. Cover and refrigerate for at least 4 hours or until thoroughly chilled.

4. Freeze your KitchenAid Ice Cream Maker bowl for 24 hours. Assemble the attachment, attach the dasher, and turn the stand mixer to "Stir" speed.

5. Pour the chilled mixture into the frozen bowl and churn for 20–25 minutes until the sorbet reaches a smooth, scoopable consistency.

6. Transfer the sorbet to an airtight container and freeze for 2–3 hours for a firmer texture before serving.

Nutritional Information (Per Serving)

- Calories: 120

- Carbohydrates: 30g

- Protein Content: 1g

- Total Fiber: 2g

- Fats: 0g

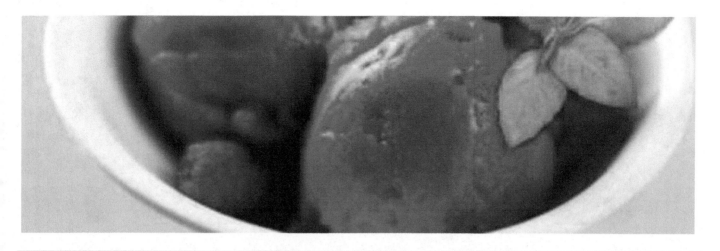

Strawberry Basil Sorbet

Time Needed to Prepare: 30 minutes (plus chilling time)
KitchenAid Time: 20–25 minutes
Servings: 6

Ingredients List

- 3 cups of fresh strawberries, hulled

- 3/4 cup of granulated sugar

- 1/4 cup of water

- 2 tablespoons of fresh basil leaves, finely chopped

- 1 tablespoon of fresh lemon juice

Instructions

1. In a small saucepan, combine the sugar and water. Heat over medium heat, stirring occasionally, until the sugar dissolves completely. Remove from heat and let the syrup cool to room temperature.

2. In a blender, puree the strawberries until smooth. Strain the puree through a fine-mesh sieve into a large bowl to remove seeds.

3. Stir the cooled sugar syrup, chopped basil, and lemon juice into the strawberry puree. Cover and refrigerate for at least 4 hours or until thoroughly chilled.

4. Freeze your KitchenAid Ice Cream Maker bowl for 24 hours. Assemble the attachment, attach the dasher, and turn the stand mixer to "Stir" speed.

5. Pour the chilled mixture into the frozen bowl and churn for 20–25 minutes until the sorbet reaches a smooth, scoopable consistency.

6. Transfer the sorbet to an airtight container and freeze for 2–3 hours for a firmer texture before serving.

Nutritional Information (Per Serving)

- Calories: 110

- Carbohydrates: 27g

- Protein Content: 1g

- Total Fiber: 2g

- Fats: 0g

Peach Bellini Sorbet

Time Needed to Prepare: 30 minutes (plus chilling time)
KitchenAid Time: 20–25 minutes
Servings: 6

Ingredients List

- 3 cups of ripe peaches, peeled and cubed

- 1/2 cup of granulated sugar

- 1/4 cup of water

- 1/2 cup of sparkling wine or prosecco

- 1 tablespoon of fresh lemon juice

Instructions

1. In a small saucepan, combine the sugar and water. Heat over medium heat, stirring occasionally, until the sugar dissolves completely. Remove from heat and let the syrup cool to room temperature.

2. In a blender, puree the peaches until smooth. Strain the puree through a fine-mesh sieve into a large bowl to remove any fibers.

3. Stir the cooled sugar syrup, sparkling wine, and lemon juice into the peach puree. Cover and refrigerate for at least 4 hours or until thoroughly chilled.

4. Freeze your KitchenAid Ice Cream Maker bowl for 24 hours. Assemble the attachment, attach the dasher, and turn the stand mixer to "Stir" speed.

5. Pour the chilled mixture into the frozen bowl and churn for 20–25 minutes until the sorbet reaches a smooth, scoopable consistency.

6. Transfer the sorbet to an airtight container and freeze for 2–3 hours for a firmer texture before serving.

Nutritional Information (Per Serving)

- Calories: 120

- Carbohydrates: 29g

- Protein Content: 1g

- Total Fiber: 1g

- Fats: 0g

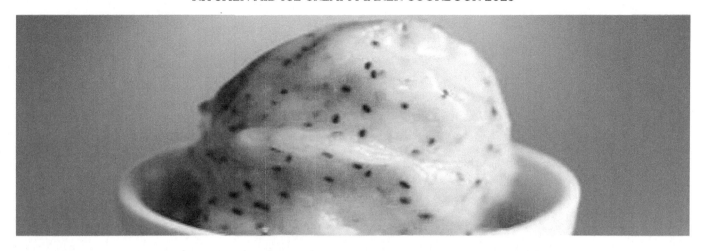

Kiwi Limeade Sorbet

Time Needed to Prepare: 25 minutes (plus chilling time)
KitchenAid Time: 20–25 minutes
Servings: 6

Ingredients List

- 6 ripe kiwis, peeled and chopped

- 1/2 cup of granulated sugar

- 1/4 cup of water

- 2 tablespoons of fresh lime juice

- Zest of 1 lime

Instructions

1. In a small saucepan, combine the sugar and water. Heat over medium heat, stirring occasionally, until the sugar dissolves completely. Remove from heat and let the syrup cool to room temperature.

2. In a blender, puree the chopped kiwis until smooth. Strain the puree through a fine-mesh sieve into a large bowl to remove seeds.

3. Stir the cooled sugar syrup, lime juice, and lime zest into the kiwi puree. Cover and refrigerate for at least 4 hours or until thoroughly chilled.

4. Freeze your KitchenAid Ice Cream Maker bowl for 24 hours. Assemble the attachment, attach the dasher, and turn the stand mixer to "Stir" speed.

5. Pour the chilled mixture into the frozen bowl and churn for 20–25 minutes until the sorbet reaches a smooth, scoopable consistency.

6. Transfer the sorbet to an airtight container and freeze for 2–3 hours for a firmer texture before serving.

Nutritional Information (Per Serving)

- Calories: 110

- Carbohydrates: 27g

- Protein Content: 1g

- Total Fiber: 2g

- Fats: 0g

Cucumber Melon Sorbet

Time Needed to Prepare: 30 minutes (plus chilling time)
KitchenAid Time: 20–25 minutes
Servings: 6

Ingredients List

- 2 cups of ripe cantaloupe or honeydew melon, cubed

- 1 cup of cucumber, peeled and chopped

- 1/2 cup of granulated sugar

- 1/4 cup of water

- 1 tablespoon of fresh lime juice

Instructions

1. In a small saucepan, combine the sugar and water. Heat over medium heat, stirring occasionally, until the sugar dissolves completely. Remove from heat and let the syrup cool to room temperature.

2. In a blender, puree the melon and cucumber until smooth. Strain the puree through a fine-mesh sieve into a large bowl to remove pulp.

3. Stir the cooled sugar syrup and lime juice into the melon-cucumber puree. Cover and refrigerate for at least 4 hours or until thoroughly chilled.

4. Freeze your KitchenAid Ice Cream Maker bowl for 24 hours. Assemble the attachment, attach the dasher, and turn the stand mixer to "Stir" speed.

5. Pour the chilled mixture into the frozen bowl and churn for 20–25 minutes until the sorbet reaches a smooth, scoopable consistency.

6. Transfer the sorbet to an airtight container and freeze for 2–3 hours for a firmer texture before serving.

Nutritional Information (Per Serving)

- Calories: 100

- Carbohydrates: 25g

- Protein Content: 1g

- Total Fiber: 1g

- Fats: 0g

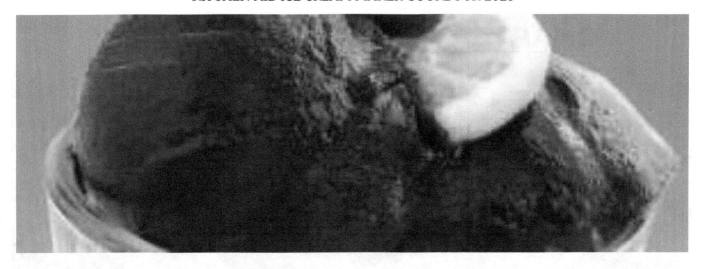

Blueberry Lavender Sorbet

Time Needed to Prepare: 30 minutes (plus chilling time)
KitchenAid Time: 20–25 minutes
Servings: 6

Ingredients List

- 3 cups of fresh blueberries (or frozen, thawed)
- 3/4 cup of granulated sugar
- 1/4 cup of water
- 1 teaspoon dried culinary lavender
- 1 tablespoon of fresh lemon juice

Instructions

1. In a small saucepan, combine the sugar, water, and dried lavender. Heat over medium heat, stirring occasionally, until the sugar dissolves completely. Remove from heat and let the syrup steep for 10 minutes. Strain to remove the lavender and let the syrup cool to room temperature.

2. In a blender, puree the blueberries until smooth. Strain the puree through a fine-mesh sieve into a large bowl to remove skins and seeds.

3. Stir the cooled lavender syrup and lemon juice into the blueberry puree. Cover and refrigerate for at least 4 hours or until thoroughly chilled.

4. Freeze your KitchenAid Ice Cream Maker bowl for 24 hours. Assemble the attachment, attach the dasher, and turn the stand mixer to "Stir" speed.

5. Pour the chilled mixture into the frozen bowl and churn for 20–25 minutes until the sorbet reaches a smooth, scoopable consistency.

6. Transfer the sorbet to an airtight container and freeze for 2–3 hours for a firmer texture before serving.

Nutritional Information (Per Serving)

- Calories: 120
- Carbohydrates: 28g
- Protein Content: 1g
- Total Fiber: 2g
- Fats: 0g

CHAPTER 4: FROZEN YOGURTS

Honey Vanilla Greek Yogurt

Time Needed to Prepare: 20 minutes (plus chilling time)
KitchenAid Time: 20–25 minutes
Servings: 6

Ingredients List

- 3 cups of plain Greek yogurt (full-fat or low-fat)
- 1/2 cup of honey
- 1/2 cup of whole milk
- 1 teaspoon pure vanilla extract

Instructions

1. In a mixing bowl, whisk together the Greek yogurt, honey, milk, and vanilla extract until smooth and fully mixed.
2. Cover and refrigerate the mixture for at least 4 hours or until thoroughly chilled.
3. Freeze your KitchenAid Ice Cream Maker bowl for 24 hours. Assemble the attachment, attach the dasher, and turn the stand mixer to "Stir" speed.
4. Pour the chilled mixture into the frozen bowl and churn for 20–25 minutes until the yogurt reaches a smooth, scoopable consistency.
5. Transfer the yogurt to an airtight container and freeze for 2–3 hours for a firmer texture before serving.

Nutritional Information (Per Serving)

- Calories: 180
- Carbohydrates: 22g
- Protein Content: 8g
- Total Fiber: 0g
- Fats: 4g

Mixed Berry Blend Yogurt

Time Needed to Prepare: 25 minutes (plus chilling time)
KitchenAid Time: 20–25 minutes
Servings: 6

Ingredients List

- 3 cups of plain Greek yogurt (full-fat or low-fat)
- 1 cup of mixed berries (blueberries, strawberries, raspberries)
- 1/2 cup of honey
- 1/2 cup of whole milk
- 1 teaspoon pure vanilla extract

Instructions

1. In a blender, puree the mixed berries until smooth. Strain the puree through a fine-mesh sieve to remove seeds.

2. In a mixing bowl, whisk together the Greek yogurt, berry puree, honey, milk, and vanilla extract until smooth and fully mixed.

3. Cover and refrigerate the mixture for at least 4 hours or until thoroughly chilled.

4. Freeze your KitchenAid Ice Cream Maker bowl for 24 hours. Assemble the attachment, attach the dasher, and turn the stand mixer to "Stir" speed.

5. Pour the chilled mixture into the frozen bowl and churn for 20–25 minutes until the yogurt reaches a smooth, scoopable consistency.

6. Transfer the yogurt to an airtight container and freeze for 2–3 hours for a firmer texture before serving.

Nutritional Information (Per Serving)

- Calories: 190
- Carbohydrates: 24g
- Protein Content: 8g
- Total Fiber: 1g
- Fats: 4g

Mango Passionfruit Yogurt

Time Needed to Prepare: 25 minutes (plus chilling time)
KitchenAid Time: 20–25 minutes
Servings: 6

Ingredients List

- 3 cups of plain Greek yogurt (full-fat or low-fat)

- 1 cup of ripe mango, peeled and cubed

- 1/2 cup of passionfruit pulp (fresh or frozen)

- 1/2 cup of honey

- 1/2 cup of whole milk

Instructions

1. In a blender, puree the mango until smooth. Strain the mango puree through a fine-mesh sieve to remove any fibers.

2. In a mixing bowl, whisk together the Greek yogurt, mango puree, passionfruit pulp, honey, and milk until smooth and fully mixed.

3. Cover and refrigerate the mixture for at least 4 hours or until thoroughly chilled.

4. Freeze your KitchenAid Ice Cream Maker bowl for 24 hours. Assemble the attachment, attach the dasher, and turn the stand mixer to "Stir" speed.

5. Pour the chilled mixture into the frozen bowl and churn for 20–25 minutes until the yogurt reaches a smooth, scoopable consistency.

6. Transfer the yogurt to an airtight container and freeze for 2–3 hours for a firmer texture before serving.

Nutritional Information (Per Serving)

- Calories: 200

- Carbohydrates: 27g

- Protein Content: 8g

- Total Fiber: 1g

- Fats: 4g

Chai-Spiced Yogurt

Time Needed to Prepare: 30 minutes (plus chilling time)
KitchenAid Time: 20–25 minutes
Servings: 6

Ingre5dients List

- 3 cups of plain Greek yogurt (full-fat or low-fat)
- 1/2 cup of honey
- 1/2 cup of whole milk
- 1 teaspoon pure vanilla extract
- 1 teaspoon ground cinnamon
- 1/2 teaspoon ground cardamom
- 1/2 teaspoon ground ginger
- 1/4 teaspoon ground cloves
- 1/4 teaspoon ground nutmeg

Instructions

1. In a mixing bowl, whisk together the Greek yogurt, honey, milk, vanilla extract, cinnamon, cardamom, ginger, cloves, and nutmeg until smooth and fully mixed.

2. Cover and refrigerate the mixture for at least 4 hours or until thoroughly chilled.

3. Freeze your KitchenAid Ice Cream Maker bowl for 24 hours. Assemble the attachment, attach the dasher, and turn the stand mixer to "Stir" speed.

4. Pour the chilled mixture into the frozen bowl and churn for 20–25 minutes until the yogurt reaches a smooth, scoopable consistency.

5. Transfer the yogurt to an airtight container and freeze for 2–3 hours for a firmer texture before serving.

Nutritional Information (Per Serving)

- Calories: 190
- Carbohydrates: 22g
- Protein Content: 8g
- Total Fiber: 0g
- Fats: 4g

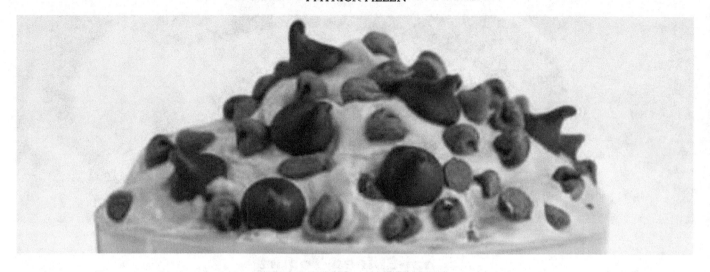

Chocolate Chip Cookie Dough Yogurt

Time Needed to Prepare: 30 minutes (plus chilling time)
KitchenAid Time: 20–25 minutes
Servings: 6

Ingredients List

- 3 cups of plain Greek yogurt (full-fat or low-fat)

- 1/2 cup of honey

- 1/2 cup of whole milk

- 1 teaspoon pure vanilla extract

- 1/2 cup of mini chocolate chips

- 1/2 cup of small chunks of edible cookie dough

Instructions

1. In a mixing bowl, whisk together the Greek yogurt, honey, milk, and vanilla extract until smooth and fully mixed.

2. Cover and refrigerate the mixture for at least 4 hours or until thoroughly chilled.

3. Freeze your KitchenAid Ice Cream Maker bowl for 24 hours. Assemble the attachment, attach the dasher, and turn the stand mixer to "Stir" speed.

4. Pour the chilled mixture into the frozen bowl and churn for 15–20 minutes until the yogurt begins to thicken.

5. During the last 5 minutes of churning, gradually add the mini chocolate chips and chunks of edible cookie dough, ensuring they are evenly distributed.

6. Transfer the yogurt to an airtight container and freeze for 2–3 hours for a firmer texture before serving.

Nutritional Information (Per Serving)

- Calories: 250

- Carbohydrates: 34g

- Protein Content: 8g

- Total Fiber: 1g

- Fats: 6g

Strawberry Banana Swirl Yogurt

Time Needed to Prepare: 30 minutes (plus chilling time)
KitchenAid Time: 20–25 minutes
Servings: 6

Ingredients List

- 3 cups of plain Greek yogurt (full-fat or low-fat)

- 1/2 cup of honey

- 1/2 cup of whole milk

- 1 teaspoon pure vanilla extract

- 1 cup of fresh strawberries, hulled and pureed

- 1 ripe banana, mashed

Instructions

1. In a mixing bowl, whisk together the Greek yogurt, honey, milk, and vanilla extract until smooth and fully mixed.

2. In a separate bowl, mix the strawberry puree and mashed banana until well mixed.

3. Cover both mixtures and refrigerate for at least 4 hours or until thoroughly chilled.

4. Freeze your KitchenAid Ice Cream Maker bowl for 24 hours. Assemble the attachment, attach the dasher, and turn the stand mixer to "Stir" speed.

5. Pour the yogurt mixture into the frozen bowl and churn for 15–20 minutes until it begins to thicken.

6. During the last 5 minutes of churning, slowly swirl in the strawberry-banana mixture, creating a marbled effect without fully mixing.

7. Transfer the yogurt to an airtight container and freeze for 2–3 hours for a firmer texture before serving.

Nutritional Information (Per Serving)

- Calories: 190

- Carbohydrates: 27g

- Protein Content: 8g

- Total Fiber: 1g

- Fats: 4g

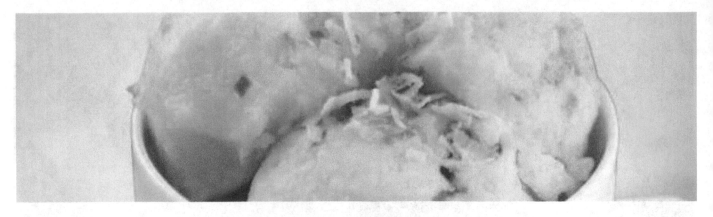

Pineapple Coconut Cream Yogurt

Time Needed to Prepare: 30 minutes (plus chilling time)
KitchenAid Time: 20–25 minutes
Servings: 6

Ingredients List

- 3 cups of plain Greek yogurt (full-fat or low-fat)

- 1/2 cup of honey

- 1/2 cup of coconut milk (full-fat)

- 1 cup of fresh pineapple, finely chopped

- 1 teaspoon pure vanilla extract

- 1/4 cup of shredded coconut, toasted (optional, for garnish)

Instructions

1. In a mixing bowl, whisk together the Greek yogurt, honey, coconut milk, and vanilla extract until smooth and fully mixed.

2. Fold in the finely chopped pineapple.

3. Cover the mixture and refrigerate for at least 4 hours or until thoroughly chilled.

4. Freeze your KitchenAid Ice Cream Maker bowl for 24 hours. Assemble the attachment, attach the dasher, and turn the stand mixer to "Stir" speed.

5. Pour the chilled mixture into the frozen bowl and churn for 20–25 minutes until the yogurt reaches a smooth, scoopable consistency.

6. Transfer the yogurt to an airtight container and freeze for 2–3 hours for a firmer texture before serving. Garnish with toasted shredded coconut if desired.

Nutritional Information (Per Serving)

- Calories: 200

- Carbohydrates: 25g

- Protein Content: 8g

- Total Fiber: 1g

- Fats: 6g

Matcha Green Tea Yogurt

Time Needed to Prepare: 25 minutes (plus chilling time)
KitchenAid Time: 20–25 minutes
Servings: 6

Ingredients List

- 3 cups of plain Greek yogurt (full-fat or low-fat)

- 1/2 cup of honey

- 1/2 cup of whole milk

- 1 1/2 teaspoons matcha green tea powder

- 1 teaspoon pure vanilla extract

Instructions

1. In a small bowl, whisk the matcha powder with 2 tablespoons of warm water until smooth and no lumps remain.

2. In a mixing bowl, whisk together the Greek yogurt, honey, milk, vanilla extract, and dissolved matcha until fully mixed.

3. Cover the mixture and refrigerate for at least 4 hours or until thoroughly chilled.

4. Freeze your KitchenAid Ice Cream Maker bowl for 24 hours. Assemble the attachment, attach the dasher, and turn the stand mixer to "Stir" speed.

5. Pour the chilled mixture into the frozen bowl and churn for 20–25 minutes until the yogurt reaches a smooth, scoopable consistency.

6. Transfer the yogurt to an airtight container and freeze for 2–3 hours for a firmer texture before serving.

Nutritional Information (Per Serving)

- Calories: 180

- Carbohydrates: 22g

- Protein Content: 8g

- Total Fiber: 0g

- Fats: 4g

Caramel Apple Crunch Yogurt

Time Needed to Prepare: 30 minutes (plus chilling time)
KitchenAid Time: 20–25 minutes
Servings: 6

Ingredients List

- 3 cups of plain Greek yogurt (full-fat or low-fat)
- 1/2 cup of caramel sauce (store-bought or homemade)
- 1/2 cup of whole milk
- 1 cup of finely chopped cooked apples (cooked with 1 tablespoon of sugar and 1/2 teaspoon cinnamon)
- 1/4 cup of granola or crushed graham crackers (for crunch)
- 1 teaspoon pure vanilla extract

Instructions

1. In a mixing bowl, whisk together the Greek yogurt, caramel sauce, milk, and vanilla extract until smooth and fully mixed.

2. Fold in the cooked apples.

3. Cover the mixture and refrigerate for at least 4 hours or until thoroughly chilled.

4. Freeze your KitchenAid Ice Cream Maker bowl for 24 hours. Assemble the attachment, attach the dasher, and turn the stand mixer to "Stir" speed.

5. Pour the chilled mixture into the frozen bowl and churn for 15–20 minutes until the yogurt reaches a smooth, scoopable consistency.

6. During the last 5 minutes of churning, add the granola or crushed graham crackers, ensuring they are evenly distributed.

7. Transfer the yogurt to an airtight container and freeze for 2–3 hours for a firmer texture before serving.

Nutritional Information (Per Serving)

- Calories: 200
- Carbohydrates: 29g
- Protein Content: 8g
- Total Fiber: 1g
- Fats: 4g

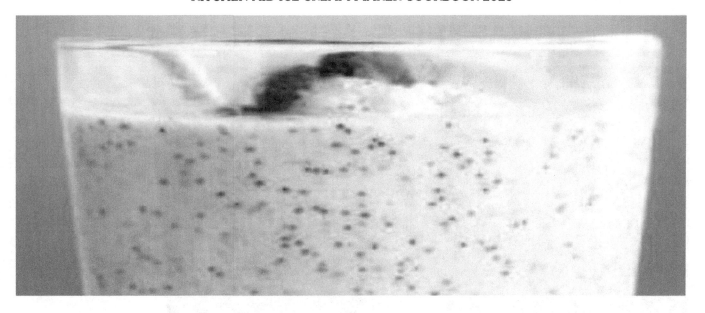

Lemon Poppy Seed Yogurt

Time Needed to Prepare: 30 minutes (plus chilling time)
KitchenAid Time: 20–25 minutes
Servings: 6

Ingredients List

- 3 cups of plain Greek yogurt (full-fat or low-fat)
- 1/2 cup of honey
- 1/2 cup of whole milk
- Zest of 2 lemons
- 1/4 cup of fresh lemon juice
- 1 teaspoon pure vanilla extract
- 1 tablespoon of poppy seeds

Instructions

1. In a mixing bowl, whisk together the Greek yogurt, honey, milk, lemon zest, lemon juice, vanilla extract, and poppy seeds until smooth and fully mixed.

2. Cover the mixture and refrigerate for at least 4 hours or until thoroughly chilled.

3. Freeze your KitchenAid Ice Cream Maker bowl for 24 hours. Assemble the attachment, attach the dasher, and turn the stand mixer to "Stir" speed.

4. Pour the chilled mixture into the frozen bowl and churn for 20–25 minutes until the yogurt reaches a smooth, scoopable consistency.

5. Transfer the yogurt to an airtight container and freeze for 2–3 hours for a firmer texture before serving.

Nutritional Information (Per Serving)

- Calories: 180
- Carbohydrates: 24g
- Protein Content: 8g
- Total Fiber: 1g
- Fats: 3g

CHAPTER 5: MILKSHAKES

Classic Chocolate Milkshake

Time Needed to Prepare: 5 minutes
KitchenAid Time: 2–3 minutes
Servings: 2

Ingredients List

- 2 cups of chocolate ice cream

- 1 cup of whole milk

- 1/4 cup of chocolate syrup (optional, for extra chocolate flavor)

Instructions

1. Assemble your KitchenAid blender or stand mixer with a blending attachment.

2. Add the chocolate ice cream, whole milk, and chocolate syrup (if using) to the blender or mixing bowl.

3. Blend on medium speed for 2–3 minutes or until the milkshake is smooth and creamy. Adjust the milk quantity for desired thickness.

4. Pour into glasses and serve immediately.

Nutritional Information (Per Serving)

- Calories: 320

- Carbohydrates: 45g

- Protein Content: 7g

- Total Fiber: 2g

- Fats: 12g

Strawberry Shortcake Shake

Time Needed to Prepare: 5 minutes
KitchenAid Time: 2–3 minutes
Servings: 2

Ingredients List

- 2 cups of strawberry ice cream

- 1 cup of whole milk

- 1/2 cup of fresh strawberries, chopped

- 1/4 cup of crumbled shortcake or vanilla cookies

Instructions

1. Assemble your KitchenAid blender or stand mixer with a blending attachment.

2. Add the strawberry ice cream, whole milk, fresh strawberries, and crumbled shortcake or cookies to the blender or mixing bowl.

3. Blend on medium speed for 2–3 minutes or until the shake is smooth and creamy. Adjust the milk quantity for desired thickness.

4. Pour into glasses and serve immediately.

Nutritional Information (Per Serving)

- Calories: 330

- Carbohydrates: 48g

- Protein Content: 7g

- Total Fiber: 2g

- Fats: 12g

Oreo Cookie Crumble Milkshake

Time Needed to Prepare: 5 minutes
KitchenAid Time: 2–3 minutes
Servings: 2

Ingredients List

- 2 cups of vanilla ice cream

- 1 cup of whole milk

- 1/2 cup of crushed Oreo cookies (plus extra for garnish)

Instructions

1. Assemble your KitchenAid blender or stand mixer with a blending attachment.

2. Add the vanilla ice cream, whole milk, and crushed Oreo cookies to the blender or mixing bowl.

3. Blend on medium speed for 2–3 minutes or until the milkshake is smooth and creamy. Adjust the milk quantity for desired thickness.

4. Pour into glasses and garnish with additional crushed Oreo cookies. Serve immediately.

Nutritional Information (Per Serving)

- Calories: 350

- Carbohydrates: 52g

- Protein Content: 8g

- Total Fiber: 1g

- Fats: 14g

Vanilla Malted Milkshake

Time Needed to Prepare: 5 minutes
KitchenAid Time: 2–3 minutes
Servings: 2

Ingredients List

- 2 cups of vanilla ice cream

- 1 cup of whole milk

- 1/4 cup of malted milk powder

Instructions

1. Assemble your KitchenAid blender or stand mixer with a blending attachment.

2. Add the vanilla ice cream, whole milk, and malted milk powder to the blender or mixing bowl.

3. Blend on medium speed for 2–3 minutes or until the milkshake is smooth and creamy. Adjust the milk quantity for desired thickness.

4. Pour into glasses and serve immediately.

Nutritional Information (Per Serving)

- Calories: 310

- Carbohydrates: 45g

- Protein Content: 8g

- Total Fiber: 0g

- Fats: 11g

Peanut Butter Banana Milkshake

Time Needed to Prepare: 5 minutes
KitchenAid Time: 2–3 minutes
Servings: 2

Ingredients List

- 2 cups of vanilla ice cream

- 1 ripe banana, sliced

- 1 cup of whole milk

- 1/4 cup of creamy peanut butter

Instructions

1. Assemble your KitchenAid blender or stand mixer with a blending attachment.

2. Add the vanilla ice cream, sliced banana, whole milk, and peanut butter to the blender or mixing bowl.

3. Blend on medium speed for 2–3 minutes or until the milkshake is smooth and creamy. Adjust the milk quantity for desired thickness.

4. Pour into glasses and serve immediately.

Nutritional Information (Per Serving)

- Calories: 360

- Carbohydrates: 42g

- Protein Content: 10g

- Total Fiber: 2g

- Fats: 16g

Mint Cookies and Cream Milkshake

Time Needed to Prepare: 5 minutes
KitchenAid Time: 2–3 minutes
Servings: 2

Ingredients List

- 2 cups of mint chocolate chip ice cream

- 1 cup of whole milk

- 1/2 cup of crushed chocolate sandwich cookies (e.g., Oreos)

Instructions

1. Assemble your KitchenAid blender or stand mixer with a blending attachment.

2. Add the mint chocolate chip ice cream, whole milk, and crushed chocolate sandwich cookies to the blender or mixing bowl.

3. Blend on medium speed for 2–3 minutes or until the milkshake is smooth and creamy. Adjust the milk quantity for desired thickness.

4. Pour into glasses and serve immediately.

Nutritional Information (Per Serving)

- Calories: 350

- Carbohydrates: 49g

- Protein Content: 7g

- Total Fiber: 1g

- Fats: 14g

Salted Caramel Toffee Milkshake

Time Needed to Prepare: 5 minutes
KitchenAid Time: 2–3 minutes
Servings: 2

Ingredients List

- 2 cups of salted caramel ice cream

- 1 cup of whole milk

- 1/4 cup of caramel sauce

- 1/4 cup of crushed toffee bits

Instructions

1. Assemble your KitchenAid blender or stand mixer with a blending attachment.

2. Add the salted caramel ice cream, whole milk, caramel sauce, and crushed toffee bits to the blender or mixing bowl.

3. Blend on medium speed for 2–3 minutes or until the milkshake is smooth and creamy. Adjust the milk quantity for desired thickness.

4. Pour into glasses and serve immediately.

Nutritional Information (Per Serving)

- Calories: 380

- Carbohydrates: 52g

- Protein Content: 7g

- Total Fiber: 0g

- Fats: 15g

Mocha Fudge Shake

Time Needed to Prepare: 5 minutes
KitchenAid Time: 2–3 minutes
Servings: 2

Ingredients List

- 2 cups of coffee ice cream
- 1 cup of whole milk
- 1/4 cup of chocolate fudge sauce (plus extra for garnish)

Instructions

1. Assemble your KitchenAid blender or stand mixer with a blending attachment.
2. Add the coffee ice cream, whole milk, and chocolate fudge sauce to the blender or mixing bowl.
3. Blend on medium speed for 2–3 minutes or until the milkshake is smooth and creamy. Adjust the milk quantity for desired thickness.
4. Pour into glasses and drizzle with additional chocolate fudge sauce. Serve immediately.

Nutritional Information (Per Serving)

- Calories: 340
- Carbohydrates: 45g
- Protein Content: 7g
- Total Fiber: 1g
- Fats: 12g

S'mores Milkshake

Time Needed to Prepare: 5 minutes
KitchenAid Time: 2–3 minutes
Servings: 2

Ingredients List

- 2 cups of vanilla ice cream
- 1 cup of whole milk
- 1/4 cup of marshmallow fluff
- 1/4 cup of crushed graham crackers
- 1/4 cup of chocolate syrup

Instructions

1. Assemble your KitchenAid blender or stand mixer with a blending attachment.

2. Add the vanilla ice cream, whole milk, marshmallow fluff, crushed graham crackers, and chocolate syrup to the blender or mixing bowl.

3. Blend on medium speed for 2–3 minutes or until the milkshake is smooth and creamy. Adjust the milk quantity for desired thickness.

4. Pour into glasses and garnish with additional marshmallow fluff or graham crackers if desired. Serve immediately.

Nutritional Information (Per Serving)

- Calories: 360
- Carbohydrates: 54g
- Protein Content: 7g
- Total Fiber: 1g
- Fats: 12g

Tropical Mango Madness Milkshake

Time Needed to Prepare: 5 minutes
KitchenAid Time: 2–3 minutes
Servings: 2

Ingredients List

- 2 cups of mango ice cream

- 1 cup of whole milk

- 1/2 cup of fresh mango, diced

- 1/4 cup of coconut cream

Instructions

1. Assemble your KitchenAid blender or stand mixer with a blending attachment.

2. Add the mango ice cream, whole milk, diced mango, and coconut cream to the blender or mixing bowl.

3. Blend on medium speed for 2–3 minutes or until the milkshake is smooth and creamy. Adjust the milk quantity for desired thickness.

4. Pour into glasses and garnish with additional diced mango or a drizzle of coconut cream if desired. Serve immediately.

Nutritional Information (Per Serving)

- Calories: 320

- Carbohydrates: 45g

- Protein Content: 6g

- Total Fiber: 2g

- Fats: 12g

MEASUREMENT CONVERSION TABLE

Measurement	Imperial (US)	Metric
Volume		
1 teaspoon	1 tsp	5 milliliters
1 tablespoon	1 tbsp	15 milliliters
1 fluid ounce	1 fl oz	30 milliliters
1 cup	1 cup	240 milliliters
1 pint	1 pt	473 milliliters
1 quart	1 qt	0.95 liters
1 gallon	1 gal	3.8 liters
Weight		
1 ounce	1 oz	28 grams
1 pound	1 lb	454 grams
Temperature		
32°F	32°F	0°C
212°F	212°F	100°C
Other		
1 stick of butter	1 stick	113 grams

CONCLUSION

As you've explored the world of homemade frozen delights, I hope this cookbook has not only inspired your creativity but also deepened your appreciation for the versatility of your KitchenAid Ice Cream Maker attachment. From creamy gelatos to refreshing sorbets, indulgent milkshakes, and tangy frozen yogurts, you now have an arsenal of recipes to transform ordinary moments into extraordinary treats.

The beauty of making your own desserts is the freedom to experiment, adapt, and create flavors that speak to your personal tastes. Whether you're hosting a party, celebrating a milestone, or simply enjoying a quiet night at home, your KitchenAid stand mixer and ice cream maker attachment have become the tools to elevate these moments.

Remember, the joy of dessert lies not just in the final scoop but in the process—the laughter in the kitchen, the anticipation as the mixture churns, and the smiles as you share your creations with loved ones. Let this cookbook be your guide and your muse, but don't be afraid to venture beyond its pages. Some of the best recipes come from bold ideas and a willingness to try something new.

Thank you for letting me be part of your culinary journey. Here's to many more bowls, cones, and shakes of joy and indulgence. Happy churning!

RECIPES INDEX

Made in United States
North Haven, CT
17 July 2025

70763428R00043